Practical

FL

(USA)

1992

Hayit Publishing

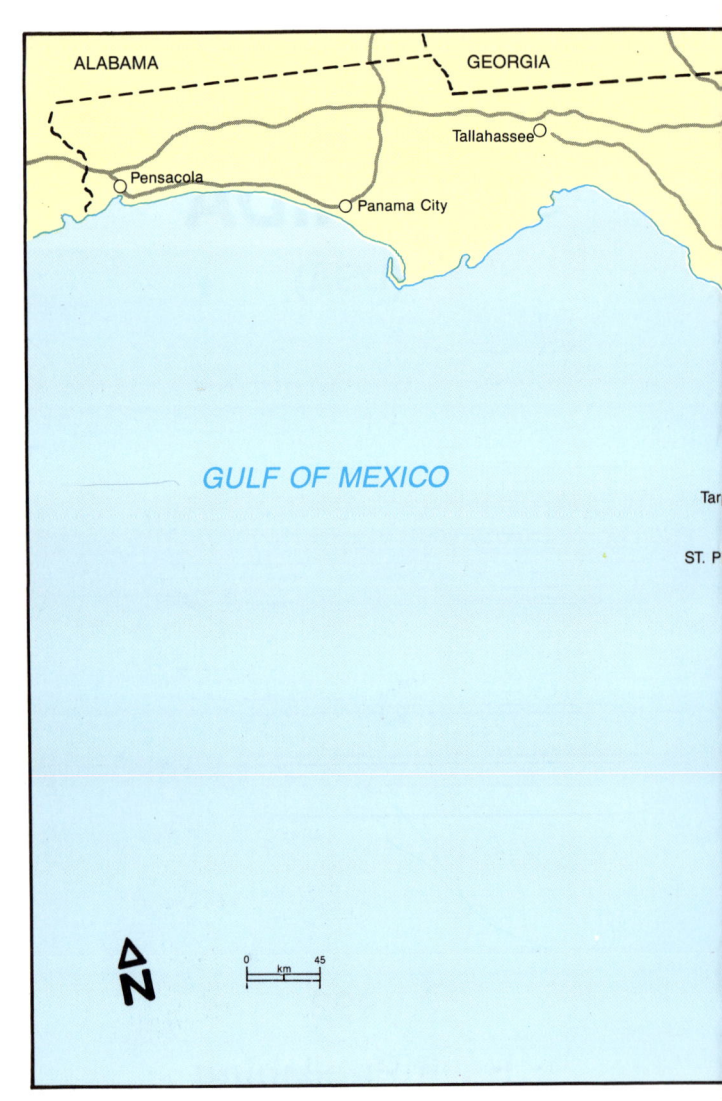

[1st] Edition 1992
UK Edition: ISBN 1 874251 30 4
US Edition: ISBN 1 56634 009 8

© copyright 1992 UK Edition: Hayit Publishing GB, Ltd, London
  US Edition: Hayit Publishing USA, Inc., New York

© copyright 1991 original version: Hayit Verlag GmbH
  Cologne/Germany

Author: Ernst Helmus
Translation, Adaption, Revision: Scott Reznik
Print: Schroff Druck, Augsburg/Germany
Coverphoto: Florida Department of Commerce
Photography: Florida Department of Commerce, Ernst Helmus, United States Travel and Tourism Administration
Maps: Ralf Tito

All rights reserved   Printed in Germany

Using this Book

Books in the *Practical Travel* series offer a wealth of practical information. You will find the most important tips for your travels conveniently arranged in alphabetical order. Cross-references aid in orientation so that even entries which are not covered in depth, for instance "Holiday Apartments," lead you to the appropriate entry, in this case "Accommodation." Also thematically altered entries are also cross-referenced. For example under the heading "Medication," there appear the following references: "Medical Care," "Pharmacies," "Vaccinations."

With travel guides from the *Practical Travel* series the information is already available before you depart on your trip. Thus, you are already familiar with necessary travel documents and maps, even customs regulations. Travel within the country is made easier through comprehensive presentation of public transportation, car rentals in addition to the practical tips ranging from medical assistance to newspapers available in the country. The descriptions of cities are arranged alphabetically as well and include the most important facts about the particular city, its history and a summary of significant sights. In addition, these entries include a wealth of practical tips — from shopping, restaurants and accommodation to important local addresses. Background information does not come up short either. You will find interesting information about the people and their culture as well as the regional geography, history and current political and economic situation.

As a particular service to our readers, *Practical Travel* includes prices in hard currencies so that they might gain a more accurate impression of prices even in countries with high rates of inflation. Most prices quoted in this book have been converted to US$ and £.

Contents

Registry of Places

Biscayne National Park	9
Cedar Key	13
Daytona Beach	17
Everglades National Park	22
The Florida Keys	25
Fort Lauderdale	27
Fort Myers	33
Homestead	39
Jacksonville	41
John F. Kennedy Space Center — Spaceport USA	44
Key Largo	46
Key West	47
Miami / Miami Beach	55
Orlando	69
Palm Beach / West Palm Beach	77
Panama City / Panama City Beach	80
Pensacola	82
Saint Augustine	86
Saint Petersburg	89
Sarasota	94
Silver Springs	100
Tallahassee	104
Tampa	106
Tarpon Springs	110
Wakulla Springs	118
Walt Disney World Resort	118
Winter Haven	123

General Information

Accommodation	7
Alcoholic Beverages	9
Automobile Club	9
Bargaining	9
Beaches	9
Camping	11
Car Rental	12
Children	14
Climate	15
Clothing	15
Crime	15
Cuisine	15
Culture	16
Customs Regulations	16
Discounts	20
Economy	20
Electricity	20
Embassies	21
Entertainment	21
Geography	36
Health Insurance	37
History	37
Holidays and Celebrations	38
Hospitals	40
Insurance	40
Literature	53
Maps and Informational Material	53
Medical Care	53
Medication	54
Money	65
Motorway Tolls	66
Nature Reserves	66
People	84
Photography	84
Police	85
Politics	85
Postal System	85
Public Transportation	85
Restaurants	86
Sales Tax	94
Shopping	96
Sights	96
Speed Limits	100
Sports and Recreation	100
Telephones	112
Theft	113
Time of Day	113
Tourist Information	113
Tourist Season	115
Traffic Regulations	115
Travel Documents	115
Travel in Florida	115
Travelling to Florida	117
Vegetation	117

Animals and Wildlife →*Nature Reserves*

Accommodation

There are numerous and good campsites for those travelling with a camping vehicle. If not travelling with a motor home or recreational vehicle, there are a number of accommodation options in various categories.

Hotels and Motels

Hotels and Motels are usually comfortably furnished and at least equipped with air conditioning and a colour television. In almost every area, there will be a selection of accommodation in various categories. At many of these, a reservation is either required or recommended.

Prices are calculated according to low and peak season and there are sometimes special rates like weekend specials. Prices for hotels begin at around $50 not including breakfast, whereas motels start for as little as $30. If a third person is travelling along, this lessens the average cost considerably since an additional person will usually pay only $5 to $8. Those who would like to travel as inexpensively as possible should ask for the price of the least expensive room.

The "Florida Hotel & Motel Travellers Guide" is available free of charge by writing to: P.O. Box 1529, Tallahassee, Florida 32302; Tel: (904) 224-2828.

Lists of especially inexpensive motel chains are available by contacting the following addresses:

Budget Hotel Inns, P.O. Box 10656, 2601 Jacksboro Highway, Suite 202, Fort Worth, Texas 76114.

Days Inns of America, 2751 Buford Highway Northeast, Atlanta Georgia 30324.

E-Z 8 Motels, 2484 Hotel Circle Place, San Diego, California 92108.

Motel 6, 51 Hitchcock Way, Santa Barbara, California 93105.

Regal 8 Inn, P.O. Box 1268, Mount Vernon, Illinois 62864.

Thrifty Scot Motels, 1 Sunwood Drive, P.O. Box 399, Saint Cloud, Minnesota 56302.

Many of the motel chains offer toll-free 1-800 numbers for further information or to make reservations.

Howard Johnson: prices range between $65 and $100 depending on location. Wellesley Inns and Park Square Inns also belong to the Howard Johnson chain, charging about 30% less. Toll-free number: 1-800-654-2000.

Best Western: prices range from $40 to $90 depending on location. Toll-free number: 1-800-528-1234.

Econolodge: prices range from $40 to $70 depending on location. Toll-free number 1-800-446-6900.

Quality Inn: prices range from $50 to $75 depending on location. Toll-free number: 1-800-228-5151.

Ramada Inn: prices range from $70 to $150 depending on location. Toll-free number: 1-800-272-6232.

Bed & Breakfast

The network of bed & breakfast inns has meanwhile spread all across the United States offering a nice alternative to the hotels and motels. A room with breakfast in private housing with or without contact with the family who runs it, offers a homey atmosphere and lends travel a different quality. Along the east coast and in Florida, the network of Bed & Breakfasts is quite extensive. Depending on the location and the distance of the bed & breakfast from principal attractions, prices for one night with breakfast range from $27 to $42.

The following address will be able to provide more information on prices and locations:

Florida Suncoast Bed & Breakfast, P.O. Box 12, Palm Harbor, Florida 33563; Tel: (813) 784-5188. Prices start at $25.

Youth Hostels

In Florida, there are not as many youth hostels as there are in other states which attract tourists. These few do, however, offer an inexpensive accommodation alternative.

Youth Hostels charge from $6 to $12 per night, given that one presents a valid international youth hostel membership card. One should, therefore, obtain a membership card before departing for Florida.

Information is available through: American Youth Hostels, National Administrative Offices, 1332 I Street, North West, Suite 800, Washington DC 20005.
→*Camping*

Guest Houses

Guest houses are yet another inexpensive alternative. These are, however, not recommended for everyone since the level of cleanliness may leave something to be desired. The prices are similar to those for youth hostels.

Alcoholic Beverages

In Florida, alcoholic beverages may only be purchased by or served to persons over the age of 21. Some alcoholic beverages can only be purchased in the liquor stores.

In addition, it is not allowed to consume alcohol or transport an open container in an automobile.

→*Cuisine, Shopping*

Automobile Club

The American Automobile Association is a partner organisation with a number of other national automobile associations throughout the world. If coming to Florida from a foreign country, membership in foreign associations often entitles members to automatic membership in the "triple A."

Those travelling by car should definitely note the 24-hour emergency number, Tel: 1-800-336-HELP.

AAA Address in Miami:

AAA, 3400 Biscayne Boulevard, Miami, Florida; Tel: (305) 573-5611.

Bargaining

In Florida, like everywhere in the United States, prices are generally set. It can, however, be the case when purchasing more expensive items like camera equipment that one can bargain with the price. If planning a trip to the Bahamas or elsewhere in the Caribbean, the opposite is quite often the case. This is also often the case with street peddlers selling handicrafts.

Beaches

The beaches of Florida require little commentary: they extend from the extreme northeastern Fernandina Beach on the Atlantic to the northwestern city of Pensacola on the Gulf of Mexico, giving Florida a total of over 8,400 miles of beaches. In addition, it is possible to swim at almost every point along the coast. There are, however, differences in the beaches, depending on one's plans and interests. The eastern coastline is impressive due to its more rugged coast and powerful surf, while the western coast has more gentle seas and soft, white sand.

Biscayne National Park

The youngest of the national parks in the United States, Biscayne National Park, given this status in 1980 in order to protect the only coral reef in the

North American continent. The park encompasses a total area of 156 square miles. It is located on Florida's southern tip about 9 miles east of Homestead and can be best reached via Canal Drive and 328th Street.

In reference to the location, the developmental conditions and geological structures, this park is directly related to the Everglades. The coastline is dominated by mangrove trees as is often the case on many of the islands. The Biscayne Bay is a preferred spawning ground for lobsters, shrimp, and schools of various types of fish and is, therefore, well protected.

Within the entire national park, especially interesting areas are marked with buoys. These also include shipwrecks like an old Spanish galleon near Elliot Key, which was discovered only a few years ago. Elliot Key is the largest of these islands about 7 miles from Convoy Point, the main entrance to the park from the coast. On Eliot Key is a small harbour as well as a visitor center, from which a 1½ mile long hiking path leads through a subtropical forest to the opposite side of the island. Especially attractive for scuba diving expeditions, the coral reef zone begins to the east of the Keys between Hawk Chan-

Miles and miles of beaches and the frothing surf — Florida ranks among the most popular destinations for aquatic sportsmen

nel and the Florida Strait. At certain times during the summer season, the turquoise waters become a playground for snorkellers and scuba divers, exploring the fascinating underwater world at a depth of up to 60 feet. Admission to the park is free of charge.

Biscayne National Park / Practical Information

Accommodation

Camping: Elliot Key Harbor, 35 sites, free of charge, accessible only by boat, groceries and supplies must be brought along; Tel: (305) 247-7275.
Boca Chita Key, simply equipped, free of charge.
→Homestead

Activities: From Convoy Point, boat excursions are offered to Elliott Key, reservations are recommended. Prices: adults $12.50; children under 12 $6; Tel: (395) 247-2400.

The park rangers' programme ranges from tours in glass-bottom boats, hiking expeditions and bird watching to introductory courses in snorkelling followed by interesting diving excursions.

Park Address: Superintendent, Biscayne National Park, P.O. Box 1369, Homestead, Florida 33090-1369; Tel: (305) 247-7275 or 247-2044.

Visitor Center: Biscayne Aqua-Center at Convoy Point. Here, one can obtain a spectrum of information on the park. The activities offered by the park rangers take place or start from here.

The visitor center is open from 9 am to 4 pm during the summer season. At Elliot Key, a smaller visitor center provides information on individual aspects of this region. It is only open on weekdays.

Weather: The summer months are humid with frequent rain showers during the afternoons. The winter months are brisk and clear.

The temperatures range between 80 and 88 °F from April until October and between 74 and 77 °F from November until May.

Camping

A total of 450 camping areas are spread across the state of Florida. These can be roughly divided into the categories of state and private camping areas. Those who chose to camp while travelling through Florida will quickly learn the difference between public and private campsites. Public campsites can be found in all of the national parks and most of the state parks. These differ from private campsites in that the fees for use are much lower and are equipped more simply. Some very modestly equipped campsites can be used free of charge, others charge a fee between $4 to $9 per tent site. As a rule, all publicly run campsites operate on a first come first serve basis, making it necessary to arrive early enough to find a vacant spot.

The private campsites, in contrast, have every amenity imaginable: washing machines, dryers, electrical hook-ups, swimming pools etc. The prices for these range from $10 to $20 for two persons per night, an additional person will pay between $2 and $4. The fees in trailer parks which are mainly for RV's can be up to $30 per night.

Reservations are accepted at all private campsites and are even required by some.

Further information is available by contacting:

Department of Commerce, Division of Tourism, 510-C Collins Building, Tallahassee, Florida 32301.

Florida Campground Association, 2329 Hampshire Way, Tallahassee, Florida 32308; Tel: (904) 893-4690.

Florida Campground Association, 1638 North Plaza Drive, Tallahassee, Florida 32308-5364; Tel: (904) 656-8878.

Car Rental

Branch offices of the larger rental agencies like Avis, Hertz, National, Budget, Alamo etc., can be found at every airport and in larger cities and towns. Interesting for foreign visitors is that these grant discounted prices when a rental car is booked from a foreign country. Such bookings can be made through automobile clubs and travel agencies.

In addition to the large agencies, there are also smaller firms, which rent out their vehicles for as little as $15 per day including tax and insurance. These firms will be listed in the local yellow pages. Often, one can get good tips in hotels, motels, at campsites and service stations. The rental vehicles from smaller firms, however, often must be returned where they were rented, whereas the larger companies allow customers to return the vehicle at any given city. One should note the following when renting a car:

- The mandatory insurance is often not sufficient; one should therefore opt for the supplemental insurance package for about $8 per day.

- The renter must be at least 21 years of age at most rental companies.

- The renter must hold a valid driving licence. For foreign visitors, a national driving licence is sufficient, but and international driving licence could speed up the process.

- Many firms will only accept the deposit for the vehicle in the form of a credit card.
- It is difficult to state exact prices because these vary from city to city. As a general rule, one should plan to spend around $140 per week on a rental vehicle.
- Those interested in especially inexpensive fares should look into the "Rent a Wreck" selection. These vehicles are a few years old, but fulfil their purpose. It is important to note that Florida is one state in the US, where liability insurance is not included in the price for a rental vehicle. Therefore, rental agents can write their own terms and conditions in the rental contract. One should read the contracts carefully. Information on this aspect is available through the AAA.
→ *Insurance*

Cedar Key

Population: 700

At the southern end of a broad arc are the group of approximately 100 islands of Cedar Key. On the largest of these islands is the fishing village of Cedar Key which formerly had an economic and strategic significance due to its harbour. Today, this is a quiet, almost sleepy fishing village with a cozy atmosphere. The main speciality in the local restaurant is, of course, seafood, whereby the smoked mullet and the swamp cabbage salad are especially worth recommending.

One can acquire more information on the city and this region in the Cedar Key Historical Society Museum and the Cedar Key State Museum. Both of these museums charge $1 admission.

Cedar Key / Practical Information

Accommodation

Motel: Beach Front Motel, $40 to $50 for one and two persons, additional person $6, reservations are recommended; Tel: (904) 543-5113.

Cedar Cove Motel, at the east end of 2nd Street, canoe rental, $45 to $60 for one and two persons, additional person $6, reservations are recommended; Tel: (904) 543-5332.

Climate: The temperatures range from 85 to 88 °F during the summer and 67 to 72 °F during the rest of the year.

Information: Cedar Key Area Chamber of Commerce, Second Street, Cedar Key, Florida 32625; Tel: (904) 543-5600.

Restaurant: The Heron Restaurant, reservations are recommended; Tel: (904) 543-5666.

Children

In many regards, Florida is not only a paradise for adults, but holds a very special attraction for children. This is not only true in the amusement parks and zoos, but along the seemingly endless coast with pleasant water temperatures. In addition, there are a number of tour agencies and even some hotels in the larger cities which offer tours especially for children. The services offered include everything from tours to parties to baby sitting and day care. Further information is available through the tourist information centers or in the yellow pages of the local telephone book.

Almost all of the admission prices are discounted for children *(→Discounts)*.

Relaxation and recreation are accentuated in Florida

Climate

Florida is the southernmost state of the continental United States, and the nickname "sunshine state" was not the result of a advertising campaign of the tourism industry — it is the simple truth. One can depend on sunshine. The winter is usually mild, although during the past few years, central and northern Florida had to deal with the consequences of frost. This took its toll on the citrus orchards to such a degree that Florida was forced to import oranges from California, their competitor in the production of citrus fruits.

In general, the temperatures in January in northern Florida will peak around 54 °F, and in the Florida Keys, they can reach up to 69 °F during the winter. The coastal regions profit especially from the warm currents of the Atlantic and the Gulf of Mexico during the winter. The temperatures in summer are quite uniform for all of Florida during the summer, averaging from 77 to 87 °F, with small variations from the northern to the southern regions.

Clothing

Florida is renowned as a holiday destination all year (→Climate). It is therefore recommended to pack light and comfortable clothing although one should also pack a warm sweater. Along the coast in the northern portion of Florida, the nights can get quite chilly, especially during the mornings and evenings. A definite must are comfortable walking shoes which can withstand an occasional hiking tour — this because of the national parks and the cities which are best explored on foot.

Crime

Despite sensational news articles about the Florida's metropolitan areas in the national and international press, crime should not hinder a pleasant visit to Florida. Tourists can do their part in lowering the crime rate by not flaunting valuables and avoiding the "less safe" areas of town during the late evening hours. In an emergency one should dial 911 for immediate assistance or dial the operator (0).
→Theft

Cuisine

The food in Florida is a reflection of the ethnic diversity of its residents (→People). In almost every city there are Chinese, Japanese, Mexican and Italian restaurants, serving good and reasonably priced food. Depending on the region one can also find Korean, Cuban, Puerto Rican, Persian, Indian, Indonesian, German and French cuisine.

Florida is world famous for the variety and quality of its seafood. Shrimp, crab, lobster, shellfish and every imaginable variety of fish is available in innumerable restaurants, especially along the coast.

Culture

When describing the culture of Florida, one must take into account the various influences that have shaped the culture of the "sunshine state."

The original Native American (Indian) culture is almost non-existent today, or stated more appropriately, it has been strongly repressed. However, those who take the effort will definitely find traces of this culture, especially in the southern regions of Florida in and around the Everglades. Presently, two large tribes live here: the Miccosukee, on the reservation on the Tamiami Trail on the northern border of Everglades National Park. The much larger Seminole population, living to the west of the Miccosukee reservation are spread among five reservations. Near Hollywood on the east coast north of Miami is a Seminole visitor center, offering information on the cultural history of the tribe. The Miccosukee tribe has set up an interesting museum west of the Shark Valley entrance to Everglades National Park, which not only offers information on the tribe's history, but on the Everglades as well.

The old Florida of the Anglo-Saxon conquers lies in the northern regions, focussing around St. Augustine. The restored streets of this, the oldest city in the United States, is reminiscent of Spain in the 16th century. Despite the truly classic beauty of this historically significant area, tourists seem to only touch upon this region. This is because most of the tourists can be found along the central belt from Busch Gardens in Tampa to the J. F. Kennedy Space Center with Orlando being the central attraction, or along the southeastern coastline from Palm Beach to Miami. This is not surprising since the dominant amusement and recreational parks as well as the entertainment centers are all concentrated in this area.

Currency →*Money*

Customs Regulations

For those arriving in Florida from countries other than the United States, it is important to note the following: before landing, a customs form must be filled out. This is an official declaration that one is bringing no more than

200 cigarettes or 50 cigars, one gallon (.375 litres) of alcoholic beverages and that the value of gifts brought along does not exceed $100.

There is no limit to the amount of currencies one is allowed to bring into Florida; however, sums in excess of $10,000 must be declared.

There are strict controls on importing plants and agricultural products. These sometimes even apply when entering other states. It is best to travel to Florida without any fresh produce, plants, etc.

Daytona Beach

Population: 55,000

The city of Daytona Beach on the Atlantic coast is located around 63 miles north of the space station Spaceport USA and the same distance from Orlando. It has gained worldwide fame through its automobile races which were first held in 1905 on the especially solid beaches measuring 23 miles in length. Today, the speed for cars on the beach is limited to 10 miles per hour. However, one can park directly by one's beach towel. The races have long since been moved to the Daytona International Speedway, but are no less popular because of it. Every year 12 large races are held on the approximately 2½ mile racetrack. Well over 100,000 visitors flock to Daytona especially during the main attractions of the Daytona 500 in February, the Paul Revere 250 on July 3rd, the Firecracker 400 on the fourth of July and other motorcycle races in March and October. The fans also populate the fairs, entertainment centers and amusement parks, of which this city has plenty: Forest Amusement Park, Mardi Gras Fun Center, the Boardwalk, the Baron Fun Frite's Castle and Ocean Front Amusements.

The 180 foot high Space Needle directly on the Boardwalk offers a beautiful view of the famous Daytona Beach.

The Museum of Arts and Sciences is located at 1040 Museum Boulevard. The exhibitions on history and natural history are especially interesting in this museum. One should plan on spending two hours in this museum.

The museum of Arts and Sciences is open Tuesdays to Fridays from 9 am to 4 pm and Saturdays and Sundays from noon to 5 pm.

Admission: $2 with free admission on Wednesdays and Saturday afternoons. The shows in the adjacent planetarium begin on Wednesdays at 3 pm, and Saturdays and Sundays at 1 and 3 pm. Especially worth recommending are the laser shows on Saturdays at 8 and 9 pm. Admission: $3, Tel: (904) 255-0285.

Daytona Beach / Practical Information

Accommodation

Camping: Daytona Beach Campground, 180 tent and RV sites, heated swimming pool, $15 to $17 for two persons, extra person $2, 4601 Clyde Morris Boulevard, reservations are recommended; Tel: (904) 761-2663.

Nova Family Campground, 525 tent and RV sites, heated swimming pool, $12 to $14 for two persons, additional person $1, 1190 Herbert Street in Port Orange, reservations are recommended; Tel: (904) 767-0095.

Orange Isles Campgrounds, 250 tent and RV sites, swimming pool, $12 to $14 for two persons, additional person $1, 3520 South Nova Road in Port Orange; Tel: (904) 767-9170.

Daytona North/Bulow KOA, Box 1328, Flagler Beach, $19 to $24 for two persons, reservations are recommended; Tel: (904) 439-2549 and 1-800-447-4KOA.

Deland/Orange City KOA, 1440 East Minnesota Avenue in Orange City, 20 miles south of Daytona Beach, 150 tent and RV sites, swimming pool, $12 to $16 for two persons, additional person $2, reservations are recommended; Tel: (904) 775-3996.

Daytona South/New Smyrna Beach, 1300 Old Mission Road, 15 miles south of Daytona Beach, heated swimming pool, $18 to $22 for two persons, additional person $4, reservations are recommended; Tel: (904) 427-3581 and 1-800-421-1KOA.

Hotels/Motels: Atlantic Waves Motel, 1925 South Atlantic Avenue, between $30 and $70 for two persons, additional person $6 to $8 (depending on the season, reservations are recommended; Tel: (904) 253-7186.

Bel-Aire Motel, 1855 South Ridgewood Avenue, $30 to $65 for two people, additional person $5 to 10 (depending on the season), reservations are recommended; Tel: (904) 767-6681.

Days Inn Interstate, 2800 Volusia Avenue, $35 to $45 for one and two persons, additional person $6; Tel: (904) 255-0541.

Esquire Motel, 422 North Atlantic Avenue, $25 to $60 for one and two persons (depending on the season), additional person $5, reservations are recommended; Tel: (904) 255-3601.

Mayfair Motel, 2232 South Atlantic Avenue, $30 to $50 for one and two persons (depending on the season), additional person $5, reservations are recommended; Tel: (904) 253-1240.

Youth Hostel: Daytona Beach Youth Hostel, 140 South Atlantic Avenue, $8 for members, Tel: (904) 258-6937.

Climate: During the summer months one can count on temperatures between 79 and 90 °F and during the winter months, temperatures range from 65 to 76 °F.

Restaurants: Asian Inn Restaurant, 2516 South Atlantic Avenue, in the Atlantic Plaza Shopping Center, reservations are recommended; Tel: (904) 786-6269.

Chart House Restaurant, 645 South Beach Street, fish specialities, reservations are recommended during weekends; Tel: (904) 255-9022.

Hungarian Village, 424 South Ridgewood Avenue, Hungarian specialities, reservations are recommended; Tel: (904) 253-5712.

Klaus' Cuisine, 144 Ridgewood Avenue, reservations are recommended; Tel: (904) 255-7711.

The Roof Restaurant, 2637 South Atlantic Avenue in the Hilton Hotel, specialising in fish, reservations are recommended; Tel: (904) 767-7350.

Transportation

Distances from Daytona Beach to:

St. Augustine — 35 miles

Orlando — 54 miles

J. F. Kennedy Space Center — 57 miles

Jacksonville — 89 miles

St. Petersburg — 100 miles

Fort Meyers — 207 miles

Fort Lauderdale — 232 miles

Miami — 257 miles

Key West — 412 miles

Pensacola — 432 miles

Airport: Daytona Beach Regional Airport (DAB), 189 Midway Avenue, Daytona Beach, Florida 32014; Tel: (904) 255-8441, approximately 3 miles west of Daytona Beach.

Important Addresses

Information: Daytona Beach Shores Chamber of Commerce, 3616 South Atlantic Avenue, Suite A, Daytona Beach Shores, Florida 32019; Tel: (904) 761-7163.

Daytona Beach Chamber of Commerce, P.O. Box 2775, Daytona Beach, Florida 32015; Tel: (904) 255-0981.

Destination Daytona, 126 East Orange Avenue, Daytona Beach, Florida 32114, Tel: (904) 255-0415.

Dog Races: Daytona Beach Kennel Club, 2201 Volusia Avenue, Daytona Beach, Florida 32015; Tel: (904) 252-6484.

Jai-Alai: Daytona Beach Jai Alai, 1900 Volusia Avenue, Daytona Beach, Florida 32014; Tel: (904) 252-0222.

The season is from the beginning of February to the beginning of August.

Automobile Races: Daytona International Speedway, P.O. Box 2801, Daytona Beach, Florida 32115-2801; Tel: (904) 253-6711.

Discounts

Students with an international or US student identification card can get discounts of up to 30% in most museums, theatres and larger aquariums, etc. Children under six will also receive discounts on admission.

Sometimes discounts are made dependent on height, an original alternative. Senior citizens, especially retirees, receive discounts similar to the students and a "Golden Age Passport" free of charge, which entitles the holder to free admission to all national parks as well as discounted fees at the campsites within the parks.

Disney World →*Walt Disney World Resort*

Economy

Florida has favourable conditions for the economy in many respects. Agriculture takes advantage of the fertile landscape and climatic conditions in the production of citrus fruits, melons, strawberries, sugar cane, vegetables as well as the breeding of livestock, especially in the area around Lake Okeechobee. The paper and wood processing industries can be predominantly found in the northern regions of Florida. Miami, Orlando and Tampa/St. Petersburg are home to large chemical and electronics firms. Orlando and Canaveral National Seashore to the east with its John F. Kennedy Space Center are a hub for the aerospace industries. Generally speaking, the electronics and high-tech industries are experiencing a boom in Florida, which can hardly be compared with any other state in the union.

Mass tourism not only brings countless visitors to Florida each year, but also an important source of income for the state. This is the most profitable branch of Florida's economy. This is not surprising when considering that Florida hosts around 40 million visitors annually.

Electricity

Those travelling to the United States from foreign countries should note that the electrical voltage is 110 volts. For this reason, it might be necessary to bring along the appropriate electrical adapters. Most laptop computers have an electrical converter chip and/or battery buffer making it necessary to only have the appropriate plug adapter.

Embassies

Canada
1746 Massachusetts Avenue, N.W.
Washington, DC 20036
Tel: (202) 785-1400

United Kingdom
3100 Massachusetts Avenue, N.W.
Washington, DC 20008
Tel: (202) 462-1340

Australia
1601 Massachusetts Avenue, N.W.
Washington, D.C. 20009
Tel: (202) 797-3000

New Zealand
37 Observatory Circle, N.W.
Washington, DC 20008
Tel: (202) 328-4800

Entertainment

Florida, with its numerous theme parks — far too many to be experienced fully in the scope of one trip to the state — can be considered America's playground. From Bush Gardens in Tampa to Walt Disney World and Epcot Center near Orlando, this state seems to be a synonym for holiday travel.
Of course, there are also other sides to Florida with its exotic landscapes, sunshine, beaches and leisure activities.
The flair of the Cuban district in Miami will enthral visitors with a rhythm and night life all its own. Miami and Miami Beach offer just about every type of entertainment imaginable from live music in the cafés and pubs to an extensive selection of bars, night clubs and discotheques. Bars and pubs seem to be enjoying a renaissance while the discotheques lose in terms of their former popularity. The centers heavily frequented by tourists have everything to offer, while other regions have their own special flair, as evident through special events and cultural attractions: the atmosphere of the Caribbean in the Florida Keys, especially Key West, is an unmistakable aspect of the night life in this region. The best way to find out where what is happening at any given time

is to page through the entertainment section of the local newspapers. Other cities have free brochures on entertainment and special events which are usually available at hotel reception desks or visitor centers.

Everglades National Park

Everglades National Park encompasses an area of almost 1.5 million acres of land and water wilderness areas, located on the southern tip of the Florida peninsula. Within the park are the Ten Thousand Islands in the northwest with Everglades City as the point of departure for this region, the Bay of Florida with the main docking point of Flamingo, and the open expanses of the Everglades. The main tourist season first begins at the beginning of December and lasts until the end of April. The reason for this is that during the remaining season, the ever-present mosquitoes become a virtual plague. The first known inhabitants of the Everglades, the Calusa Indians, called this area of wild reeds and grasses in the seemingly endless swamp "Pa-Hay-Okee," which translates as "flowing grass." This grass landscape, similar to a prairie, dominates the northeast portion of the park; to the south there is an increasing number of small but dense pine and cypress groves. The broad coastline then has lush grove of various types of mangroves, which are among the few types of land plants which can grow in saltwater. Presently, these interesting plants lead to the fact that the southern tip of Florida is constantly increasing in area — a few square yards every year — extending into the Gulf of Mexico and the Florida Bay.

A typical characteristic will draw the visitor's attention: the so-called *Hammocks,* small islands of vegetation. Growing on these islands are tropical evergreen forests, although these regions are within a tropical climatic zone. This botanical peculiarity of the hammocks is accessible at two points within the park: the Gumbo Limbo Trail and at the even more beautiful Mahogany Hammock. Both are located in the Flamingo Zone. Pineapples and orchids grow on these islands among the tangled branches of the larger trees. Parasitic plants wrap themselves around the larger trunks, gradually "choking" their host in the mutual battle for light. Later, the parasitic plants are destine to fall victim in the same way to other competitors. Stages of this battle for survival, typical for a tropical jungle, can be observed at the hammocks.

These small, tropical forests offer the land animals sufficient food when they retreat to these islands during the rainy season. In total, this unique area pro-

---

A favourite in Florida: the airboat tours through Everglades National Park ▶

ves to be a paradise for countless species of animals and of course for the millions of aquatic birds. Among at least three hundred species of birds which are indigenous to Everglades National Park is the meanwhile endangered national bird of the United States, the bald eagle. Still living in the extensive swamp areas are also the manatees — large clumsy looking sea lions. Remaining to be mentioned is the growing population of alligators, which are among the more than one hundred species of amphibians and reptiles represented in Florida. Along the 38 mile long park road from the main entrance to Flamingo, there are various educational hiking trails which branch off into several regions and landscapes.

From Flamingo, there are bicycle and hiking trails varying in length from 4 to 15 miles. In addition, canoe routes make an impressive and memorable means of exploring the Everglades. A trip along the 100 mile long Wilderness Waterway from Flamingo to Everglades City is especially impressive. When travelling at a relatively high speed with a motor boat, this route takes 6 to 8 hours. Day-long tours covering this route are also offered. If attempting this route in a canoe, one should allow 6 to 7 days.

Everglades National Park / Practical Information

Accommodation

Camping: Flamingo Campground, 295 tent and RV sites, $7; Tel: (305) 247-6211. Long Pine Key Campground, 108 tent and RV sites, $7; Tel: (305) 247-6211. Both campgrounds can usually be used during the off season free of charge. Within the park are an additional 20, simply equipped campsites which can also be used free of charge. These are, however, only accessible on foot or by boat.

Reservations for the campgrounds can only be made for groups and can be place through the Superintendent's Office (→*Important Addresses, this entry*).

Motel and Cottages: Flamingo Inn, in the town of Flamingo, peak season $60 for two persons, apartments for up to four persons $100, additional person $6, cottages from $50, with reduced prices during the off season. Information: Flamingo Inn, Flamingo, Florida 33030; Tel: (305) 253-2241 and (813) 695-3101.

Canoe Rental: Everglades Canoe Outfitters, 39801 Ingraham Highway, Homestead, Florida 33034; Tel: (305) 246-1503.

Climate: During the winter, the weather is dry and clear with temperatures around 76 °F. The summer months can be rainy and sometimes stormy with temperatures reaching from 87 to 92 °F.

Maps: US Coast and Geodetic Survey, Washington, D.C. 20240.

Medical Care: All of the ranger stations are equipped for first aid. The nearest hospital is located in Homestead, 12½ miles from the main entrance to the park and 48 miles from Flamingo.

Restaurants: There is a restaurant in Flamingo. It is, however, closed during the summer.

Visitor Centers: Parachute Key Visitors Center at the main entrance, open 8 am to 5 pm, good informational materials, also available in foreign languages.

Royal Palm Interpretive Center at the beginning of the Anhinga and Gumbo Limbo trails, open 8 am to 5 pm, ranger programme also available; Tel: (305) 247-6211.

Visitor Center in Flamingo, including a museum; Tel: (305) 695-3101.

Shark Valley Visitor Center in the northeastern portion of the park; Tel: (305) 2218776.

Visitor Center in Everglades City, a little over a half a mile south of town on State Route 29.

Ranger Station in Flamingo; Tel: (305) 247-6211, and in Everglades City; Tel: (813) 695-3311.

Admission: the admission at the main entrance is $5 per vehicle or $3 per person; at the Shark Valley Entrance, $3 per vehicle or $1 per person.

Important Addresses

Superintendent Everglades National Park, P.O. Box 279, Homestead, Florida 33030; Tel: (305) 247-6211.

One can also order nautical maps by contacting this address.

The Florida Keys

The Florida Keys begin in the outskirts of Miami with Virginia Key between Miami and Key Biscayne and extend over 181 miles to Dry Tortugas, only 91 miles from Cuba. The 114 mile long Overseas Highway 1, which connects the various sized coral and mangrove islands through 42 bridges, leads 50 miles southwards from Miami near Jewfish Creek to the first oblong island of Key Largo. This scenic route ends in Key West which is still 69 miles from Dry Tortugas.

For a long time, the residents of these islands made their living from "wrecking," that is to say from salvaging from shipwrecks. The reason for this was that a number of ships from the Spanish fleet were stranded or shipwrecked on the Florida Keys when transporting gold and other goods from Mexico and Peru to the homeland. Today, there are still several "wreckers" who have made this into their profession. Among them are Mel Fisher, the manager of Treasure

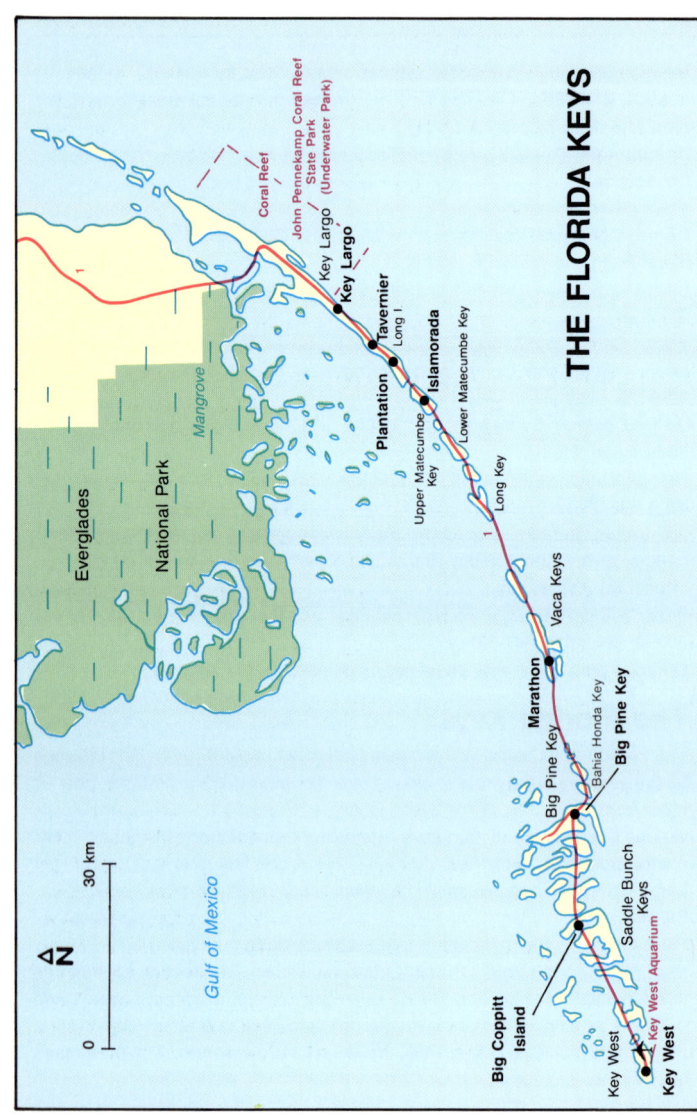

Salvors Inc., who is accredited with finding the Atocha treasure in 1985 — an event which made the rounds through the international press. His excursions were based in Key West. He also exhibits interesting objects found during his treasure hunts in a museum located there.
→*Biscayne National Park, Key Largo, Key West*

Fort Lauderdale

Population: 155,000

The name of the lively city of Fort Lauderdale originates from Major William Lauderdale, who established a fort here in 1838 on the banks of New River during the Seminole War.

Those who visit Fort Lauderdale will understand why the city is also called "the Venice of Florida." Seemingly endless canals and rivers run through the city. Approximately 165 miles of the over 188 miles of waterways are accessible by boat. It is therefore not surprising that in this paradise of waterways, countless boating hobbyists feel right at home. Meanwhile, there are over 30,000 boats and yachts of all shapes and sizes in Fort Lauderdale. This figure is only surpasses by the number of college students who visit Fort Lauderdale during the Christmas and Easter seasons. Fifty thousand students flock to Fort Lauderdale at these times — a tradition which has been upheld since 1960 when the bestseller "Where the Boys Are" was filmed in this city. Since then, students make for a lively atmosphere and dominate the beach which measures over 6 miles. The activities of the students have meanwhile become established as an attraction in Fort Lauderdale.

Fort Lauderdale / Sights

Atlantis, The Water Kingdom, 2700 Stirling Road in Hollywood. This aquatic park with wave pools, water slides and various shows is one of the largest of its kind in the United States. A day ticket costs $14 for adults and $11 for children from 3 to 7 years of age, parking fee per vehicle $2; Tel: (305) 926-1000.

Discovery Center, 231 Southwest 2nd Avenue. This former hotel "New River Inn" in the older portion of the city now houses a museum of history and science. Visitors have access to hands-on exhibits and can observe how various things function. Open from September to May from noon to 5 pm; June to August 10 am to 5 pm, Saturdays 10 am to 5 pm, Sundays noon to 5 pm, closed Mondays. Admission is $3 for adults; $2.50 for seniors and free of charge for children under 3 years of age. Information on guided tours and special programmes: Tel: (305) 462-4115.

Everglades Holiday Park Airboat Tours, 21940 Griffin Road. The tours on these propeller driven air boats through the outer regions of the Everglades is one of the main attractions in this park. There is also alligator wrestling. Open daily from 9 am to 5 pm.

A boat tour costs $12 for adults, $6 for children from four to twelve years of age; Tel: (305) 434-8111.

International Swimming Hall of Fame, 1 Hall of Fame Drive. Displayed here is everything worth knowing about the sport of swimming and a good deal of information on former and current swimming stars — From Ester Williams to Mark Spitz and Greg Louganis. Those who have more than a few hours to spend can take a dip in the adjacent Olympic sized swimming pool (if training or swimming competitions do not happen to be taking place). Admission: $3 for adults, students up to 21 years of age $1; Tel: (305) 462-6536. Swimming pool: Tel: (305) 523-0994.

Ocean World, 1701 Southeast 17th Street Causeway. Trained dolphins and sea lions perform their tricks here. Visitors can feed the dolphins or observe the sharks being fed. There are also a number of alligators. In addition, there is an extensive area with apes and parrots. Open daily from 10 am to 6 pm. Admission: $10 for adults, $8 for children from four to twelve years of age. Tel: (305) 525-6611.

Although rodeo is a sport most common in the western states of America, there are still a few in Florida. One is near Fort Lauderdale in the city of Davie. Every Friday, the *Friday Night Rodeo* is held at the rodeo grounds on Davie Road.

Seminole Okalee Indian Village, 6031 Stirling Road in Hollywood. Life in the Indian Village has been adapted to tourism with dances, alligator wrestling and much more. The Seminole Tribal Fair and Rodeo takes place during February in this village. Information on prices and programmes: Tel: (305) 583-3590.

State Parks: In the direct vicinity of Fort Lauderdale there are two state parks. At 3109 East Sunrise Boulevard on the Atlantic Coast is the Hugh Taylor Birch State Recreation Area (Tel: (305) 564-4521) and somewhat further to the north of the city at 6503 North Ocean Drive is the John U. Lloyd Beach Recreation Area. These are only partially developed reef islands where one can swim or scuba dive; Tel: (305) 928-2833.

Fort Lauderdale / Practical Information

Accommodation

Camping: Candlelight Park Campground, 500 tent and RV sites, heated swimming pool, $18 to $22 for two persons, additional person $1, 5731 State Road 7S, reservations are recommended; Tel: (305) 791-5023.

John D. Easterlin Park Campground, 55 tent and RV sites, $14 per site, 1000 Northwest 38th Street; Tel: (305) 776-4466.

Kozy Kampers Travel Trailer Park, priced from $20 for two person, 3631 West Commercial Boulevard, reservations are recommended; Tel: (305) 731-8570.

Markham Park Campground, 86 tent and RV sites, from $18 to $20 per site, 16001 West State Road 84; Tel: (305) 384-7004.

Trinity Towers RV Park, 187 RV sites, $15 to $20 for two persons (depending on the season), additional person $2, heated swimming pool, reservations are recommended, 3300 Pembroke Road, in Hollywood; Tel: (305) 962-7400.

Hotels/Motels: Days Inn/Downtown, 1700 West Broward Boulevard, $40 to $70 for one and two persons (depending on the season), additional person $6, reservations are recommended; Tel: (305) 463-2500.

Hampton Inn, 720 East Cypress Creek Road, $45 to $62 for one and two persons (depending on the season), additional person $6; Tel: (305) 776-7677.

Imperial Apartment Motel, 3054 Harbor Drive, $36 to $74 for two persons, additional person $8 to $10 (depending on the season), reservations are recommended; Tel: (305) 525-1533.

Climate: During the winter months, the weather is fresh and clear; the summer brings warm, humid weather with regular rain showers during the afternoon. The temperatures reach 87 to 92 °F in summer and during the winter they can still reach 78 °F.

Medial Care: The Medical Association offers consultation services or they can suggest physicians; Tel: (305) 525-1595.

Night Life and Entertainment: Mai-Kai, →*Restaurants, this entry.*

The larger hotels will almost always have bars with live entertainment. In addition, there are a number of clubs and discotheques in the downtown area, in Oakland Park in the northern part of the city and along the beach.

The brochure "Guide to the Gold Coast Sun Spots" contains information on the current programme. Other good sources of information are the daily newspapers "Fort Lauderdale News" and "Sun Sentinel."

Restaurants: Casa Vecchia, 209 North Birch Road, specialising in Italian cuisine, excellent wine list, reservations are recommended; Tel: (305) 463-7575.

The Down Under, 3000 East Oakland Park Boulevard, a restaurant with an exclusive flair, excellent wine list, reservations are recommended; Tel: (305) 563-4123.

Gerd Müller's Ambry, 3016 East Commercial Boulevard, good steaks and lamb cutlets; Tel: (305) 771-7342.

Mai-Kai, 3599 North Federal Highway, excellent Polynesian restaurant, specialising in duck dishes, reservations are recommended. This is also a good place to spend the evening. The Polynesian Revue is excellent. Tel: (305) 563-3272.

Shopping: A number of shops and stores can be found on Goldenrod Road and on Dr. Phillips Boulevard. A stroll through the older part of the city, Himmarshee Village, is definitely worthwhile as is walking down the Oceanwalk in Hollywood.

Sightseeing

The largest sightseeing tour agencies are:

Greyline; Tel: (305) 587-8080, and

Greyhound Bus Tours; Tel: (305) 764-6551.

Other agencies include:

American Sightseeing Tours, Inc., 740 Southwest 158th Lane, Sunrise, Florida 33326; Tel: (305) 463-4805.

Dolphin Limousine Service, Inc., 2307 Hollywood Boulevard, Hollywood, Florida 33020; Tel: (305) 989-5466.

Red Top Sedan Service, Inc., 740 Southwest 158th Lane, Sunrise, Florida 33326; Tel: (305) 463-4805.

The "Voyager Train City Tour" leads eight miles through the interesting streets and boulevards of Fort Lauderdale. The price for the one and one-half hour tour is $6.50 for adults, $6 for seniors and $3 for children from 3 to 11 years of age. The tour begins at 600 South Seabreeze Avenue directly opposite the Bahia Yacht Club. A number of combined tours are also offered. Information: Tel: (305) 463-3149 or (305) 463-0401.

Sightseeing tours by boat:

Jungle Queen, Bahia Mar Yacht Basin, 801 Seabreeze Boulevard. The sightseeing trip on New River lasts about three hours including a one hour visit to the Indian Village. Departs daily at 10 am and 2 pm; Prices: $6.95 for adults and $4.95 for children under 12. There is also a barbeque dinner cruise departing at 7 pm. Price including dinner is $20.95. Information and reservations: Tel: (305) 462-5596.

America's Venice: Fort Lauderdale is a Mecca for amateur captains ▶

Paddlewheel Queen, 2950 Northeast 32nd Avenue. There are various tours offered from sightseeing to luncheon cruises on this Mississippi riverboat. Information and reservations: Tel: (305) 564-7659.

Sports and Recreation

Boating: Owing to the favourable conditions in Fort Lauderdale, this sport has advanced to one of the most popular. In almost all of the larger ports, there are boat rental agencies.

Fishing: The fishing conditions attract countless fishermen from near and far. Appropriate equipment as well as fishing boats are available at Pier 66 and at Marina del Americana.

Golf: Reservations for golf can often be made in the hotels. Some hotels have agreements with a golf course to allow their guests the use of these courses. Check at the reception desk.

Dog Races: Hollywood Kennel Club, 831 North Federal Highway, in Hallandale; Tel: (305) 758-3646. Races take place from December through April.

Jai Alai: 301 East Dania Beach Boulevard, in Dania; Tel: (305) 949-2424 or (305) 927-2841.

Horse Races: Gulfstream Park, 901 South Federal Highway, in Hallandale; Tel: (305) 944-1242 or (305) 454-0399. The season is from the beginning of January to May.

Tennis: Public tennis courts can be found in Holiday Park; Tel: (305) 761-5378; in George English Park; Tel: (305) 566-0622; and in Sunland Park; Tel: (305) 761-5406.

Transportation

Trains: Amtrak Station, 200 Southwest 21st Street; Tel: (305) 463-8251.

Buses: The public bus routes operated by the Broward County Transportation Authority serve the greater Fort Lauderdale area. Information: Tel: (305) 357-8400.

Greyhound Terminal: 515 Northeast 3rd Street; Tel: (305) 764-6551.

Continental Trailways Terminal: 130 Northwest 1st Avenue; Tel: (305) 463-6327.

Distances from Fort Lauderdale to:

Miami — 25 miles
Fort Myers — 134 miles
St. Petersburg — 148 miles
J. F. Kennedy Space Center — 167 miles
St. Augustine — 178 miles
Key West — 180 miles
Orlando — 205 miles
Daytona Beach — 232 miles

Jacksonville — 320 miles
Pensacola — 638 miles
Air Travel: The Fort Lauderdale/Hollywood International Airport is located at 1400 Lee Wagener Boulevard, approximately 4½ miles from the center of town. For $6 to $8, one can make use of the shuttle service operating between the airport and the downtown area.
Airport Information: Tel: (305) 357-6100.
Taxi: The taxi fares average around $1.75 for the first mile and $1.20 for each additional mile.

Important Addresses
Broward County Hotel/Motel Association, 1212 Northeast 4th Avenue, Fort Lauderdale, Florida 33304; Tel: (305) 462-0409.
Greater Fort Lauderdale Chamber of Commerce, 208 Southeast 3rd Avenue, Fort Lauderdale, Florida 33301; Tel: (305) 462-6000.
The Greater Fort Lauderdale Convention and Visitors Bureau, 500 East Broward Boulevard, Suite 104, Fort Lauderdale, Florida 33394; Tel: (305) 765-4466.
Greater Hollywood Chamber of Commerce, 330 North Federal Highway, Hollywood, Florida 33020; Tel: (305) 920-3330.

Fort Myers

Population: 37,000
An exotic landscape as well as a healthy climate have made Fort Myers famous. This reputation is also the result of the famous discoverer of the light bulb and the phonograph: Thomas Alva Edison, when he built a winter residence here in 1886 at the age of 39 on recommendation of his physician. Edison lived to the ripe age of 84. After visiting Fort Myers, many are convinced of the positive aspects of this region. Supplementing this are not only the renovated inner city of Fort Myers and the lush vegetation but also the exotic aspects of the islands off the coast: Sanibel, Captiva, Estero and Pine among others.

Fort Myers / Sights

Thomas A. Edison Winter Home and Gardens, 2350 McGregor Boulevard. The famous discoverer lived in this house up until his death in 1931. The botanical gardens, measuring 14 acres in area, were laid out by Edison himself. Tours through the house, the garden and the museum are very interesting. Open Monday to Saturday from 9 am to 4 pm, Sundays 12:30 to 4 pm. Admission: adults $6, $2 for children from 6 to 12 years of age. Information: Tel: (813) 334-3614; group tours: Tel: (813) 334-7419. Combined tickets for the Edison and Ford estates (see below): adults $8, children from 6 to 12 years of age $3.

Henry Ford Winter Home. Another famous resident and neighbor of Thomas Edison in Fort Myers was the industrialist Henry Ford. His house has been restored using photographic records. A friendship developed between Ford and Edison — one of the main reasons for Ford to purchase this house. Tours of this winter estate are available either singly or in combination with tours of the Edison estate. For information, contact the numbers listed above. Admission: adults $4, children from 6 to 12 years of age $2.

Shell Factory, 2787 North Tamiami Trail in North Fort Myers. This museum exhibits an extensive collection of shells and corals in all colours and forms. Tours are offered free of charge. One should allow one hour to visit this museum. Open from 9:30 am to 6 pm; Tel: (813) 995-2141.

Waltzing Waters, 18101 US 41 Southeast. This park includes special attractions like water shows, concerts and laser light shows.

Open daily from 11 am to 9 pm. Admission: $7.50 for adults, $3.50 for children from 7 to 12 years of age. Information: Tel: (813) 267-2533.

For those interested in seashells and corals, a visit to the islands off the coast will prove to be an unforgettable experience.

Fort Myers / Practical Information

Accommodation

Camping: Fort Myers Beach RV Resort, 300 tent and RV sites, heated swimming pool, $18 for two persons, additional person $1.50, 16299 San Carlos Boulevard in Fort Myers Beach, reservations are recommended; Tel: (813) 466-7171, within Florida: 1-800-FLA-CAMP.

Gulf Air Travel Park, 240 tent and RV sites, heated swimming pool, $16 to $18 for two persons, additional person $2, 17279 San Carlos Boulevard in Fort Myers Beach, reservations are recommended; Tel: (813) 466-8100.

Shady Acres Travel Park, 325 tent and RV sites, swimming pool, $16 for two persons, additional person $1, 19370 South Tamiami Trail, reservations are recommended; Tel: (813) 267-8448.

Woodsmoke Camping Resort, 300 tent and RV sites, from $18 for two persons, additional person $2, heated swimming pool, 19251 US 41 Southeast, about 9 miles south of Fort Myers, reservations are recommended; Tel: (813) 267-3456.

Hotels/Motels: Days Inn South/Airport, 11435 Cleveland Avenue, $30 to $70 for one and two persons (depending on the season), additional person $4, reservations are recommended; Tel: (813) 936-1311.

Knights Inn, 13251 North Cleveland Avenue, $40 to $60 for one and two persons (depending on the season), additional person $3; Tel: (813) 656-5544.

Rock Lake Motel, 2930 Palm Beach Boulevard, $30 to $50 for one and two persons (depending on the season), additional person $3; Tel: (813) 334-3242.

Car and RV Rental: Cruise America, 2549 Cleveland Avenue, Fort Myers, Florida 33901; Tel: (813) 337-0306.

Sunburst RV Center, 1295 North Tamiami Trail, North Fort Myers, Florida 33903; Tel: (813) 656-0900.

U-Haul Company, 11401 Cleveland Avenue, Fort Myers, Florida 33907; Tel: (813) 939-3686.

Restaurants: Mariner's Inn, 3448 Marinatown, specialising in fish dishes, reservations are recommended; Tel: (813) 997-8300.

The Shallows, 5833 Winkler Road, also offering live entertainment on occasion, reservations are recommended; Tel: (813) 481-4644.

The Veranda, 2122 2nd Street, closed Sundays, reservations are recommended; Tel: (813) 332-2065.

Sightseeing: Royal Palm Tours, Inc., P.O. Box 06079, Fort Myers, Florida 33906; Tel: (813) 489-0344.

Sun Lines, P.O. Box 06626, Fort Myers, Florida 33906; Tel: (813) 337-0600.

Sunrise Enterprises of Southwest Florida, 2780 South Street, P.O. Box 06626, Fort Myers, Florida 33906; Tel: (813) 337-0600.

Transportation

Distances from Fort Myers to:

St. Petersburg — 69 miles

Ft. Lauderdale — 134 miles

Miami — 145 miles

Orlando — 154 miles

John F. Kennedy Space Center — 188 miles

Daytona Beach — 207 miles

St. Augustine — 250 miles

Key West — 180 miles

Jacksonville — 285 miles

Pensacola — 550 miles

Airport: Southwest Florida Regional Airport (RFW), 16000 Chamberlin Parkway Southeast, Fort Myers, Florida 33913; Tel: (813) 768-1000.

The airport is approximately 10 miles southeast of the city.

Important Addresses

Chamber of Southwest Florida, P.O. Box 1290, 1365 Hendry Street, Fort Myers, Florida 33902; Tel: (813) 334-1133.

Lee County Visitor and Convention Bureau, P.O. Box 2445, Fort Myers, Florida 33902; Tel: (813) 335-2631.

Geography

The predominantly flat peninsula of Florida makes up the southernmost tip of the continental United States, separating the Atlantic Ocean from the Gulf of Mexico with a total area of 58,560 square miles. The entire coastline measures over 8440 miles, whereby the western coast south of the Suwannee River is interrupted by large bays.

Florida, especially the southern regions of the state, alternated between being below and under the water level with the alternating warm periods and ice ages during the past 500,000 years. This allowed for the thick sedimentary limestone layers. Visitors can still see this geologically significant evidence at some points where white stone shimmers through the water, only inches deep in some areas. Flowing through these limestone layers today is a huge shallow freshwater river which encompasses almost the entire breadth of the Everglades. Its source is to be found at the Okeechobee Lake around 240 miles from the southern tip of Florida.

Due to the minimal slope from the north to the south, this river is only a few inches deep, flowing extremely slowly. This is also a reason for discovering the climatic and geological interdependency in Florida — a discovery which was almost made too late:

In order to make the land arable, the people dug canals and controlled the water levels by building dikes around the expansive land areas as well as the Okeechobee Lake, which is now a huge freshwater reservoir. A dike between Tampa and Miami cut off the natural and essential flow of water to the Everglades. In the subsequent years, the land increasingly dried up and the bountiful rainfall, so essential for the agriculture, decreased drastically and the population of aquatic birds also showed a dramatic decline.

It was only in the beginning of the 1980's that the responsible officials began to cut back on the dike building projects in order to reestablish the natural water cycle. One hundred sixty-six rivers and over three thousand lakes, make for a high fish population in the waters of Florida. Most of the lakes are in the central regions of Florida from the northern Lake City to Lake Okeechobee. The vegetation is extremely diverse, which is not surprising given the optimal climatic conditions. Especially in the northern regions, there are expansive pine forests as well as oaks and cypresses; in the southern regions, the characteristic palm trees become apparent. Fifteen different species of palms grow in Florida. Finally, in the swamp areas, the extensive mangrove forests make up a type of natural labyrinth.

Health Insurance

Payment for medical and dental treatment is expected in advance, although insufficient funds is not a reason for refusing treatment in emergencies. A credit card can definitely be helpful with large sums for treatment. It is also recommended to take out a supplemental travel health insurance policy for the duration of one's trip. Most major insurance companies and some airlines and credit card companies offer such policies. Travel insurance is usually quite reasonably priced and are limited to the exact dates of travel.
→Money, Insurance

History

If tracing Florida's history — or more specifically, its settlement — back to its origins, one will skip over a period of approximately ten to twelve thousand years. The Indians were the first to arrive in Florida after having immigrated from Siberia, coming through Alaska and continuing deeper into the warmer regions around the end of the ice age. They finally arrived at this peninsula. Directly at the beginning of the first settlement of Florida through European conquerors (These included predominantly Spaniards in addition to the French and English), at the beginning of the 16th century they were confronted by embittered resistance by the Indian population. The Calusa Indians, who lived as nomads, hunting and fishing in the fertile landscape, could withstand the attacks for around 200 years, until their ultimate demise finally became inevitable.

Up to around the turn of the century, the northern portion of this peninsula counted as the civilised portion of Florida, while the rest was wilderness and considered fit only for alligators, the Indians and only a few courageous settlers. A turn came with Henry P. Plant and Henry M. Flagler. Both of these men have gone down in history as pioneers of the railroad in Florida. Plant connected both coasts through central Florida leading to Tampa with his Atlantic Coast Line, while Flagler's Florida East Coast Railway went into service for the eastern coastal route in 1896. In 1912, this route extended from Jacksonville in the north all the way to Key West in the south.

Florida continued to develop at an ever increasing rate. Today, this state is among the most advanced in terms of the economy and in terms of tourism. This is also the result of the favourable climatic and natural conditions.

Holidays and Celebrations

The national holidays are usually observed on a Monday, making it possible for many to take a short trip during the long weekend. Visitors should avoid the main highways, national parks and recreation areas on these days because they will always be extremely congested.

National Holidays:
January 1: New Year's Day;
Third Monday in January: Martin Luther King Jr.'s Birthday;
Third Monday in February: President's Day (celebrating George Washington's and Abraham Lincoln's Birthdays);
Easter Sunday;
Last Monday in May: Memorial Day;
July 4: Independence Day;
First Monday in September: Labor Day;

Today, a portion of the Seminole Indians live on reservations

Second Monday in October: Columbus Day;
Fourth Monday in October: Veterans' Day;
Fourth Thursday in November: Thanksgiving Day;
December 25: Christmas Day.
Public offices, post offices, most banks and museums are closed on these days. On official holidays, with the exception of Easter, Christmas and New Year's Day, many stores remain open.
In addition, there are a number of unofficial holidays, special events and festivals, for which there are no set dates.

Holiday Apartments →*Accommodation*

Homestead

Population: 21,000
The city of Homestead is a centre for fruit production in southern Florida. Numerous stands along the roadside are not only evidence for the importance of this economic sector, but they are also a good place to purchase these quality products at reasonable prices. In regard to tourism, Homestead has a favourable geographical location as a point of departure for trips to the Everglades and Biscayne National Park as well as to the Florida Keys.

Homestead / Sights

One of the main attractions in Homestead is the *Coral Castle,* 28655 South Federal Highway. During the period from 1920 to 1940, Ed Leedskalnin built this fascinating castle from 1,000 tons of coral and only using primitive tools. Open daily from 10 am to 9 pm. Admission: $7.75 for adults and $4.50 for visitors from 7 to 15 years of age; Tel: (305) 248-6344.
Not far from Homestead is the *Orchid Jungle (→Miami).* Fruit, nuts and various vegetation from almost every tropical region around the globe can be seen at the *Preston B. Bird and Mary Heinlein Redland Fruit and Spice Park.* Open daily from 10 am to 5 pm, 24801 Southwest 187th Avenue; Tel: (305) 247-5727.

Homestead / Practical Information

Accommodation

Camping: Chekika State Recreation Area, 20 tent and RV sites, $6 for four persons, located on Southwest 237th and Grossmann Drive; Tel: (305) 253-7400. Goldcoaster Motorhome and RV Park, 547 tent and RV sites, $17 for two persons, additional person $1, 34850 Southwest 187th Avenue; Tel: (305) 248-5462.

Hotels/Motels: Everglades Motel, 605 South Krome Avenue $28 to $40 for one and two persons, additional person $5; Tel: (305) 247-4117.
Holiday Inn, 990 Homestead Boulevard, $35 to $65 for one and two persons (depending on the season), additional person $10; Tel: (305) 247-7020.
Coral Roc Motel, 1100 North Krome Avenue in Florida City, $30 to $50 for one and two persons, additional person $4; Tel: (305) 247-4010.
Scottish Inn, 1223 Northeast 1st Avenue in Florida City, $35 to $60 for one and two persons (depending on the season), additional person $4; Tel: (305) 247-6621.

Important Addresses

Greater Homestead/Florida City Chamber of Commerce, 60 US Highway 1, Homestead, Florida 33030; Tel: (305) 247-2332.

Hospitals

In Florida, there is a hospital in almost every city, providing high standards in medical care. In addition, almost every national park has first aid stations. Many of the larger cities will have medical and dental referral services, which will be able to recommend physicians and dentists.
→*Medical Care, Health Insurance*

Insurance

There are travel insurance policies available, covering just about everything. Minimum travel coverage should include travel health, accident and baggage insurance. These can often be combined into a relatively inexpensive insurance package which is limited to the exact dates of travel.

If one should require treatment in a hospital or clinic, payment is expected in cash or by credit card. Treatment costs range from $400 to $600 per day, which makes not only a credit card handy in this situation, but an insurance policy which covers these costs as well.

This is also true in the case of travel liability insurance. The liability insurance included in most travel packages does not cover liability to the owner, holder or driver of a motorised vehicle, aircraft or motorised boat, due to damages resulting from the use of the vehicle. This makes it wise to opt for the additional insurance coverage available when renting a vehicle. Depending on the company, this ranges from $8 to $18 per day. Without this, coverage is usually limited to only $25,000.

Further information is available through insurance companies, automobile clubs or the American Underwriters and the AAA, which are represented in most larger cities in the United States.
American International Underwriters, 70 Pine Street, New York, New York 10005.
American Automobile Association, Travel Insurance Department, 8111 Gatehouse Road, Falls Church, Virginia 22047.

Jacksonville

Population: 541,000

The St. Johns River which flows through Jacksonville is the only river in Florida which flows to the north. Its filthy appearance makes a vivid impression of the heavy industry in Jacksonville. The city claims to be the largest in the United States in terms of area and is a major commercial center with factories, a harbour, trains, large financial institutions and impressive insurance buildings. An attraction in the center of town is the Friendship Fountain with a colourful water spectacle taking place every evening. Other than this, the coastal road A1A is the most interesting route. It leads to Beach Pier and the Boardwalk at Jacksonville Beach or to Little Talbot Islands State Park north of Fort George Island. However, the A1A is usually used to access Kingsley Plantation Historic Site at 11676 Palmetto Avenue, approximately 3¼ miles north of the St. Johns River ferry docks on the northern shores of Fort George Island. This former slave plantation was one of the oldest in the state of Florida. The plantation complex, slaves' quarters and the manor house can be toured. Admission: $1; Information: Tel: (904) 251-3122.

Jacksonville / Practical Information

Accommodation

Camping: Jacksonville South/St. Augustine KOA, 125 tent and RV sites, $18 to $23 for two persons, additional person $3 to $4, 9950 Koa Road; Tel: (904) 824-8309.
Little Talbot Island State Park, 40 tent and RV sites, $10 for four persons, 17 miles north of the A1A; Tel: (904) 251-3231.
Hotels/Motels: Best Inns of America, 8220 Dix Ellis Trail, $30 to $36 for one and two persons, additional person $4; Tel: (904) 739-3323.
Days Inn Airport, 1153 Airport Road, $28 to $36 for one and two persons, additional person $5; Tel: (904) 757-5000.
Red Carpet Inn, 5331 West University Boulevard, $28 for one and two persons; Tel: (904) 733-8110.

Jacksonville

Restaurants: Crawdaddy's, 1643 Prudential Drive, specialising in fish dishes, reservations are recommended; Tel: (904) 396-3546.

RV Rental: American Recreational Vehicles, Inc., 1117 Beach Boulevard, Jacksonville Beach, Florida 32250; Tel: (904) 249-8602.

Ryle Tucker Co., 5521 Blanding Boulevard, Jacksonville, Florida 32210; Tel: (904) 771-7300.

Sun Coast RV Center, 9945 Beach Boulevard, Jacksonville, Florida 33216; Tel: (904) 642-1600.

Shopping: Jacksonville Landing is a shopping center which is heavily frequented by tourists. It is located on the northern banks of the St. John River. Information: Two Independent Drive, Jacksonville, Florida 32202; Tel: (904) 353-1188.

Sightseeing: Florida North, Inc., P.O. Box 8834, Jacksonville, Florida 32239; Tel: (904) 721-2422.

Grey Line of North Florida, 6034 Richard Street, Jacksonville, Florida 32216; Tel: (904) 730-2232.

A World of Travel, 313 West Ashley Street, Jacksonville, Florida 32202; Tel: (904) 355-7245.

Transportation

Distances from Jacksonville to:

St. Augustine — 24 miles
Daytona Beach — 89 miles
St. Petersburg — 131 miles
Orlando — 134 miles
J. F. Kennedy Space Center — 154 miles
Ft. Myers — 285 miles
Ft. Lauderdale — 320 miles
Miami — 327 miles
Pensacola — 360 miles
Key West — 500 miles

Airport: Jacksonville International Airport (JAX), P.O. Box 18097, Jacksonville, Florida 32229; Tel: (904) 741-2000.

The airport is located approximately ten miles north of the city. It has recently been expanded and modernised, increasing its significance in the air travel network.

The construction of Spaceport USA complex spurred vigorous conflict between conservationists and scientists ▶

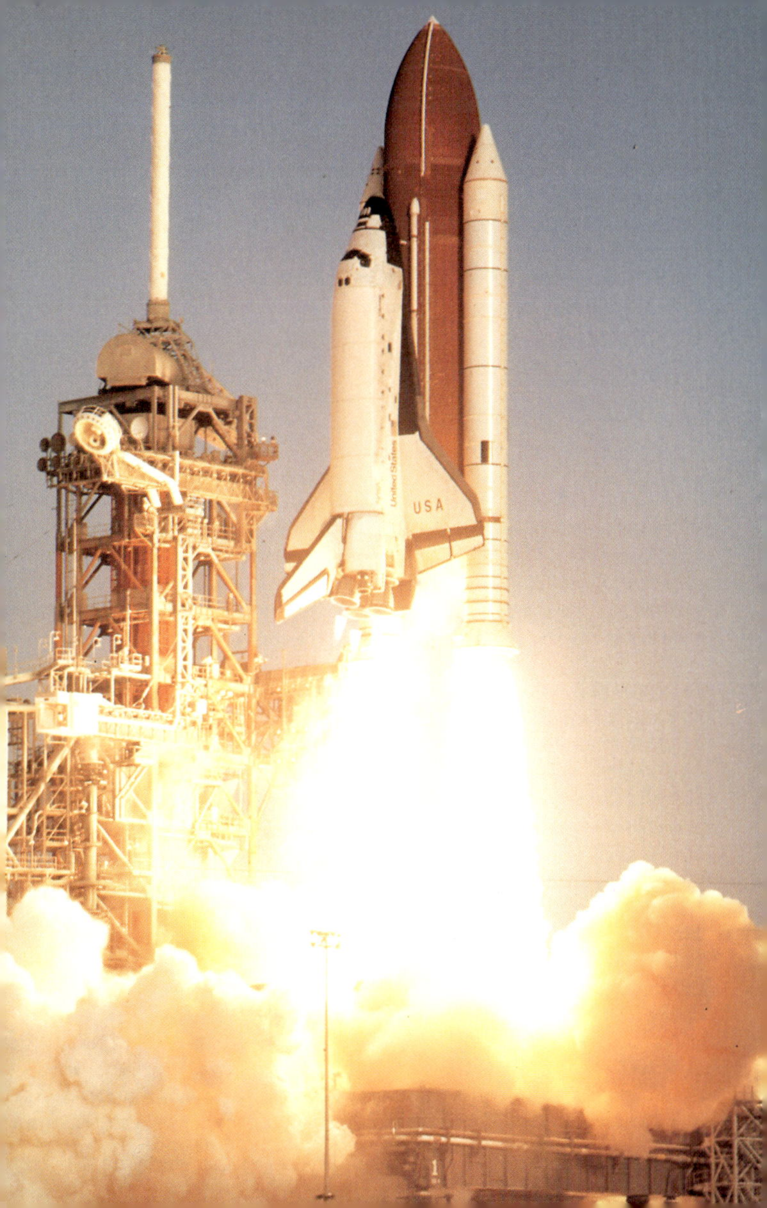
USA
United States

Important Addresses

Jacksonville and its Beaches Convention & Visitors Bureau, 6 East Bay Street, Suite 200, Jacksonville, Florida 32202; Tel: (904) 353-9736.

Jacksonville Chamber of Commerce, 3 Independent Drive, Jacksonville, Florida 32201; Tel: (904) 353-0300.

John F. Kennedy Space Center / Spaceport USA

The NASA (National Aeronautics and Space Administration) was founded in 1958 in answer to the "Sputnik Shock." In this region, however, the NASA was not greeted with open arms because an almost untouched landscape would fall victim to this development. Nature conservationists demanded that a nature reserve be established, which would protect this landscape from the ambitious plans of mankind. A compromise which allowed for both views was finally reached. Spaceport USA is located amid two nature reserves encompassing a total of almost 225 square miles: the Merritt Island National Wildlife Refuge and the Canaveral National Seashore. Skepticism among the conservationists quickly disappeared when it was discovered that the animals were not driven away by the "intruders" or by the deafening sound of a launch. Obviously, a place has been developed where nature and technology can coexist in harmony.

The Canaveral National Seashore has meanwhile been given the status of national park. Information: P.O. Box 6447, Tutusville, Florida 33090; Tel: (407) 267-1110.

Living in this nature reserve are the majestic bald eagles, the national bird on the United States coat of arms, as well as ospreys, vultures, storks, brown and white pelicans, beautiful egrets, and a number of other migratory species of birds. Giant turtles also lay their eggs on this beach, undisturbed by humans, but definitely by their natural predators: raccoons and armadillos. Living in the waters off the coast are alligators and the meanwhile rare manatees, the famous sea cows of Florida. From Titusville, two roads (State Roads 406 and 402) lead to the headquarters of this nature reserve including an informative visitor center. Interest is, however, mainly directed toward the space center which has an expansive visitor center, providing a great deal of information and orientation. Located near the parking area in Rocket Garden with its numerous types of rockets, a spacecraft and a lunar lander, the visitor center is equipped with a number of exhibition and lecture halls in which films are shown documenting the successes of NASA. Celebrated in the aerospace center in 1989, the

20th anniversary of the first landing on the moon served as an occasion for the NASA to make the visitor center more attractive. There are now three new attractions which have been opened in the aerospace station, offering visitors new perspectives (free of charge). These begin with "The Boy from Mars," a short science fiction film; continues with "Satellites and You," a highly entertaining visit to a space station of the future; and finally includes the astronaut memorial monument. Touring these exhibitions in the visitor center is still offered free of charge. There are, however, admission charges of $2.75 for adults and $1.75 for children from 3 to 12 for the IMAX Theater. Here, a film of a space shuttle launch leaves quite an impression as does the two hour tour through the space center complex on board a 106 seater double-decker bus. When visiting the John F. Kennedy Space Center/Spaceport USA, one should allow a minimum of four to five hours. Open daily from 9 am to dusk; tours are offered from 9:45 am until two hours before dusk.

John F. Kennedy Space Center / Practical Information

Accommodation

Camping: Cocoa/Cocoa Beach KOA, $19 for two persons, additional person $2, 820 Barnes in Rockledge, reservations are recommended; Tel: (407) 636-3000 or 1-800-541-8420.

Titusville KOA, $18 to $20 for two persons, additional person $2 to $3, 4513 West Main Street in Mims, reservations are recommended; Tel: (407) 269-7361 or 1-800-848-4562.

Space Center Campground, 272 tent and RV sites, $16 to $18 for four persons, additional person $2, 7275 US1 South near Titusville; Tel: (407) 269-0947.

Jetty Park Campground, 117 tent and RV sites, $16 to $20 for six persons, 400 East Jetty Road; Tel: (407) 783-7297.

Ameri-Cana Resort Co-op, Inc., 417 sites, no tents, $18 to $22 for two persons, additional person $2, 6700 US Highway 1 near Cocoa; Tel: (407) 259-4599.

Hotels/Motels: Best Western Cocoa Inn in Cocoa, 4225 West King Street, $40 to $50 for one and two persons; Tel: (407) 632-1065.

Econo Lodge Beachside, 5500 North Atlantic Avenue in Cocoa Beach, $45 to $55 for one and two persons (depending on the season), additional person $4; Tel: (407) 784-2550.

Best Western Space Shuttle Inn, 3455 Cheney Highway in Titusville, $45 to $55 for one and two persons, additional person $4; Tel: (407) 269-9100.

Rodeway Inn, 3655 Cheney Highway in Titusville, $45 to $55 for one and two persons, additional person $4; Tel: (407) 269-7110.

Along the Cheney Highways are a number of other inexpensive motels.

Transportation

Distances from John F. Kennedy Space Center to:

Orlando — 47 miles

Daytona Beach — 65 miles

St. Augustine — 117 miles

St. Petersburg — 142 miles

Jacksonville — 154 miles

Fort Lauderdale — 167 miles

Miami — 188 miles

Fort Myers — 191 miles

Key West — 342 miles

Pensacola — 472 miles

Important Addresses

Kennedy Space Center's Spaceport USA, TWRS Kennedy Space Center, Florida 32899; Tel: (407) 452-2121.

Titusville Area Chamber of Commerce, 2000 South Washington Avenue, Titusville, Florida 32780; Tel: (407) 267-3036.

Key Largo

Population: 7,400

Key Largo, the longest of the Florida Keys measuring 30 miles in length is especially renowned for its underwater park "John Pennekamp Coral Reef State Park." Directly on the beach is an visitor center an abundance information on the park.

This state park was the first underwater park in the United States and includes a portion of the only living coral reef in North America in its 78 square miles. Also belonging to the state park is a small beach and a little off the coast, slightly below the shallow water is the 10 foot tall bronze statue, "Christ of the Deep." Those who do not consider this much of an attraction will find compensation in the two and a half hour trip in a glass-bottom boat or by taking a snorkelling or scuba diving expedition. Boat excursions cost $14 for adults and $7 for children from 3 to 11 years of age. Reservations are recommended; Tel: (305) 451-1202.

There is also a boat rental agency for those wishing to tour the region independently by boat. This is located directly next to the visitor centre. If there is a wait for one of these boats, one can stroll along the wooden planks through the extensive groves of mangrove trees.

Key Largo / Practical Information

Accommodation

Camping: John Pennekamp Coral Reef State Park, 47 tent and RV sites, $12 for four persons; Tel: (305) 451-1202.
Calusa Camp Resort, from $18 for two persons, 325 Calusa Road on US 1, swimming pool, reservations are recommended; Tel: (305) 451-0232 or (305) 248-7525.
America Outdoors, 154 tent and RV sites, $18 to $20 for two persons, additional person $2, Route 1, P.O. Box 38A, reservations are recommended; Tel: (305) 852-8054.
Hotels/Motels: Holiday Inn on US 1, mileage marker 100, $65 to $95 for one and two persons (depending on the season), additional person $6; Tel: (305) 451-2121.

Important Addresses

John Pennekamp Coral Reef State Park, P.O. Box 487, Key Largo, Florida 33037; Tel: (305) 451-1202.
Key Largo Chamber of Commerce, 103400 Overseas Highway, Suite 235, Key Largo, Florida 33037; Tel: (305) 451-1414.

Key West

Population: 25,000

With the exception of cities on the Hawaiian Islands, Key West — at the end of the Overseas Highway — is the southernmost city in the United States. This is emphasised by a colourfully painted stone at the southern edge of the city with the inscription on the adjacent wall: "90 miles to Cuba." The geographical location and the Caribbean influence has always been a trademark of this city. Before this area was developed and before the arrival of the first long-term residents, this area served as a secure hide-out. This area was then later transformed into a base for defence against the pirates.

During the middle of the 19th century, this island and the entire region were characterised by such prosperity that Key West became the city with the largest per capita income in the United States. This prosperity is still evident from several magnificent villas, some of which are completely covered with tropical vegetation all the way up to their roofs. In some places, nature appears to even be winning in the battle for living space, where massive trees take up almost the entire front gardens and the beautiful buildings seem to be threatened with constraint. The tropical vegetation is an integral part of Key West and is characterised by impressive diversity — a paradise for those exploring the city on foot. They will be able to observe this diversity and experience the intense fragrance of blossoming trees, bushes and flowers, becoming sensitised to nature.

Due to the almost palpable proximity to the sugar cane islands and also because of its tropical flair, Key West has become a second home for many of the Cubans living in exile, who in turn, inevitably intensify the Cuban character of Key West. This influence can be seen everywhere and is apparent in everything including the cuisine with conch chowder, black beans with rice, arroz con pollo (rice with chicken), turtle steak and keylime pie being among the specialities in the characteristic cafés and restaurants in Key West. The atmosphere in Key West is incredibly stimulating. This could have been the reason that Tennessee Williams ("Streetcar Named Desire"), Earnest Hemingway ("For Whom the Bell Tolls"), Robert Frost and so many other authors and artists were attracted to this city.

Those who travel to Key West should not merely breeze through this city. One should at least spend one evening here and experience the dancers, musicians, magicians, amateur actors and other colourful activity on Mallory Pier, while awaiting the famous sunset with other curious tourists with a romantic bent. Afterwards, the night life kicks into gear in the various pubs and traditional bars of Key West.

Key West / Sights

Aquarium, 1 Whitehead Street. The Aquarium dates back to the 1930's and offers insight into the underwater world of the Florida Keys. Open daily from 10 am to 6 pm; admission $5.50 for adults, $2.75 for visitors from 8 to 15 years of age. Tel: (305) 296-2051.

Audubon House, corner of Whitehead and Greene Street, 205 Whitehead Street. A villa with a garden definitely worth seeing, this once belonged to the famous naturalist and artist John James Audubon. Admission: $5 for adults, $1 for children from 6 to 12 years of age. Open from 9:30 am to 5 pm; Tel: (305) 294-2116.

Duval Street, the main commercial and shopping street with several residential houses and buildings from the 1820's and 1830's.

East Martello Tower, gallery and museum, 3501 South Roosevelt Boulevard. This stone fortress from the civil war now houses an art gallery and various memorabilia from old Key West. Admission for adults is $3, visitors from 7 to 15 years of age $1; Information: Tel: (305) 296-3913.

Earnest Hemingway House and Museum, 907 Whitehead Street. In this house with its magnificent garden, the Nobel prize winning author lived and worked for ten years, composing some of his most significant novels including "For Whom the Bell Tolls" and "A Farewell to Arms." Today, this magnificent villa has been converted into a museum, offering a fascinating perspective of the life of this author. Open daily from 9 am to 5 pm; admission: $6 for adults, $1.50 for children from 6 to 12 years of age. Tel: (305) 294-1575.

Lighthouse and Military Museum, 938 Whitehead Street. From the lighthouse, one has a spectacular panorama over Key West. An interesting exhibit in the museum is a two-man Japanese submarine captured in Pearl Harbor. Open daily from 9:30 am to 5 pm; admission $4 for adults, $1 for visitors from 6 to 16 years of age. Tel: (305) 294-0012.

Mel Fisher Maritime Heritage Company, 3840 North Roosevelt Boulevard. Interesting exhibits pertaining to this famous treasure hunter. Open daily from 10 am to 6 pm; admission: $5 for adults, $1 for children from 6 to 12 years of age. Information: Tel: (305) 296-4444.

Oldest House Museum, 322 Duval Street. This is a house built in 1829. It now houses the Wreckers' Museum with models of old ships. Open daily from 10 am to 4 pm; admission: $2 for adults and 50 cents for children from 3 to 12 years of age. Information: Tel: (305) 294-9502.

Key West / Practical Information

Accommodation

Camping: Boyd's Camping, 130 tent and RV sites, from $20 for two persons, 6401 Maloney Avenue, located near the beach, reservations are recommended; Tel: (305) 294-1465.

Jabour's Trailer Court, 90 tent and RV sites, from $22 for two persons, additional person $3, bicycle rental, 223 Elizabeth Street, located in the direct vicinity of the old city, reservations are recommended; Tel: (305) 294-5723.

Hotels/Motels: Blue Marlin Motel, 1320 Simonton Street, $45 to $90 for one and two persons (depending on the season), additional person $12; Tel: (305) 294-2585.

Santa Maria Motel, 1401 Simonton Street, $40 to $90 for one and two persons (depending on the season), additional person $12; Tel: (305) 296-5678.

Southernmost Motel, 1319 Duval Street, $45 to $90 for one and two persons (depending on the season), additional person $10; Tel: (305) 296-6577.

Youth Hostel: Key West Hostel, 1125 Unites Street, $10 during the summer and $12 during the winter for members; Tel: (305) 296-5719.

Beaches: The beach is located on the Atlantic side of Key West. Shower facilities are also available at the beach.

Night Life and Entertainment: Of all of the many bars and pubs in this city, Captain Tony's Saloon at 420 Greene Street, known as Hemingway's Bar, is the most famous. During the times of this great romancer, the bar was still called Sloppy Joe's. Now, another bar, located only a few steps away, has this name. These are meeting places for young people who enjoy good live music. Much more stylish and exclusive is the atmosphere in the Hotels Casa Marina at 1500 Reynold Street and Pier House Inn at 1 Duval Street. One usually meets the upper crust of the city in these locales offering live music. It is interesting to compare these two completely different styles of night life when strolling through Key West during the late evening hours.

Restaurants: Bagatelle, 115 Duval Street, Caribbean cuisine; Tel: (305) 294-7195.

Buttery, 1208 Simonton Street, expensive but excellent; Tel: (305) 294-0717.

Crab Shack, 908 Caroline Street, fish dishes, often serving all you can eat specials during the evening, inexpensive.

Lighthouse Cafe, 917 Duval Street, Italian cuisine, inexpensive; Tel: (305) 296-7837.

Queens Table Dining Room, 1401 Simonton Street in the Santa Maria Motel, reservations are recommended; Tel: (305) 296-5678

Turtle Kraals, on the corner of Caroline and Margaret Street, specialising in fish and seafood, reasonable prices. A visit to this restaurant is also worth while because of the various fishponds on the premises. There is also an additional pool for the giant turtles.

Shopping: In the "Shell Warehouse," on Mallory Square are shells in every imaginable shape, colour and size, which can also be purchased as a souvenir; Tel: (305) 294-5168.

Sightseeing: Conch Tour Train, 601 Duval Street. These small, open streetcars take passengers past about 60 points of interest during the one and a half hour tour. Departures daily from 9 am to 6 pm, $11 for adults and $5 for children from 4 to 15 years of age. Information: Tel: (305) 294-5161.

Fireball Glass Bottom Sightseeing Boat, 2 Duval Street. During a two-hour tour, this boat takes passengers to the living coral reef. Departures daily from 8 am to dusk, adults $14 and children from 3 to 12 years of age $7. Information: Tel: (305) 296-4160 or (305) 296-6923.

CENTRAL KEY WEST

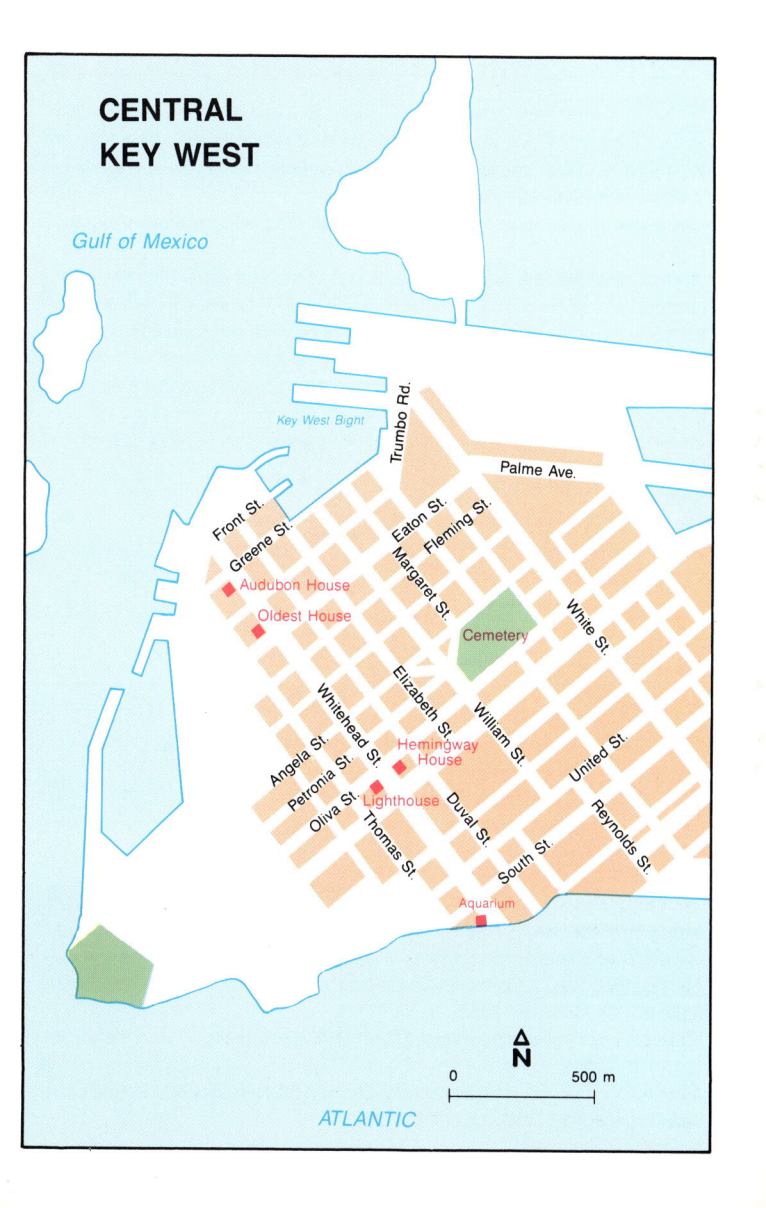

Gulf of Mexico

Key West Bight

Front St.
Greene St.
Trumbo Rd.
Palme Ave.
Eaton St.
Fleming St.
Margaret St.
White St.

Audubon House
Oldest House
Cemetery

Whitehead St.
Angela St.
Petronia St.
Oliva St.
Elizabeth St.
William St.
United St.
Reynolds St.

Hemingway House
Lighthouse
Thomas St.
Duval St.
South St.

Aquarium

N
0 500 m

ATLANTIC

The Old Town Trolley, 1910 North Roosevelt Boulevard, takes passengers on a tour through the old districts of Key West. Departures daily from 8:55 am to 4:30 pm, $12 for adults and $5 for children from 4 to 12 years of age. Information: Tel: (305) 296-6688.

Seaplane Tours offered by the Key West Seaplane Service include flights to Dry Tortugas.

Sports and Recreation: On Duval Street, there is a store which rents out bicycles. Prices are $8 to $10 per day and $35 to $40 per week. From December to the beginning of May, Berenson Pari-Mutuel holds greyhound racing. Information: Tel: (305) 294-9517.

Various recreational activities are offered on Mallory Square Dock — from sailing to snorkelling and scuba diving.

Boats depart from City Marina (Roosevelt Boulevard) on deep-sea fishing excursion.

Transportation

Distances from Key West to:

Miami — 129 miles
Fort Lauderdale — 180 miles
St. Petersburg — 239 miles
Fort Myers — 274 miles
St. Augustine — 289 miles
John F. Kennedy Space Center — 342 miles
Orlando — 372 miles
Daytona Beach — 413 miles
Jacksonville — 500 miles
Pensacola — 800 miles

Airport: Key West International Airport (EYW), 3492 South Roosevelt Boulevard; Tel: (305) 296-5439. The airport is located approximately 2 miles east of the city.

Important Addresses

The Key West Welcome Center is located at 3840 North Roosevelt Boulevard. Here, one can obtain maps and informational materials. One can even rent bicycles and boats. Information: Tel: (305) 296-4444.

Greater Key West Chamber of Commerce, 402 Wall Street, Key West, Florida 33040; Tel: (305) 294-2587.

The Florida Keys and Key West, P.O. Box 464, Key West, Florida 33041; Tel: (305) 296-2228.

Monroe County Tourist Development Council, P.O. Box 866, Key West, Florida 33041-0866; Tel: (305) 296-2228.

Literature

Key West, a resident to three masters of American Literature, prompts the recommendation of the following works:

Robert Frost, *Poetry.*
Earnest Hemingway, *A Farewell to Arms,* (1929).
Earnest Hemingway, *For Whom the Bell Tolls,* (1940).
Tennessee Williams, *Dramas.*

Maps and Informational Material

Maps and informational materials are available free of charge from the tourist and information bureaus, the visitor centers and the chambers of commerce in individual cities.

If entering Florida from Georgia and/or Alabama, one will notice the so-called welcome centers shortly after the border. These also have good informational material. The materials are usually city maps, road maps and suggested routes or information providing an orientation in regard to the various attractions, national parks and nature reserves.

Road maps are available from the triple A *(→Automobile Club)* or they can be purchased at service stations.

By contacting the following addresses, one can also request useful information. Some of these organisations do, however, charge a fee. One should also contact these addresses well in advance.

Florida Division of Tourism, 126 Van Buren Street, Tallahassee, Florida 32399-2000; Tel: (904) 487-1462.

Florida Chamber of Commerce, P.O. Box 11309, Tallahassee, Florida 32302; Tel: (904) 222-2831.

Special Attractions in Florida: P.O. Box 833, Silver Springs, Florida 32688; Tel: (904) 694-5444.

Florida Automobile Information, Division of Tourism, Direct Mail Section, 107 West Gaines Street, Tallahassee, Florida 32304.

Historical Sites: Department of State, Division of Archives, History and Records Management, The Capitol, Tallahassee, Florida 32301; Tel: (904) 487-2333.

For information on special events: Department of Commerce, Division of Tourism, 510-C Collins Building, Tallahassee, Florida 32301.

Medical Care

The standards of medicine in Florida are excellent. Payment for medical and dental treatment is expected immediately in cash or by credit card *(→Money),*

making a travel health insurance policy recommendable (→Health Insurance). Most larger cities will have a medical and dental referral service listed in the telephone book. They will be able to recommend general physicians and specialists depending on what treatment is required.
Almost all of the National Parks are equipped with a medical clinic or at least a first aid station.
→Medication

Medication

Due to the intensity of the sun, it is a good idea to pack sun lotion with a high protection factor as well as lip balm. Insect repellent is a must for a trip into the Everglades because of the mosquitoes which can be quite an annoyance. These articles are also readily available in supermarkets and drug stores within Florida.

More then a museum: the famous American writer Ernest Hemingway lived and worked in this house

If one takes specific medications on a regular basis, these should be brought along; this is especially true for foreign visitors since the composition of a given medication can vary.
→*Medical Care*

Miami / Miami Beach

Population: 1.7 million

There are two theories regarding the origin of the city's name. According to the first, the name Miami comes from the Native American language "Lake of Mayaime," a word in the Tequesta Indian language for "fresh or sweet water." According to the other theory, the geographical references of "Ayami" or "Mayami" have evolved into "Miami." These old names were on old Spanish maps, after they landed near Miami for the first time in the 17th century. When Henry Flagler's "Florida Eastcoast Railway" was completed all the way

Captain Tony's Saloon was formerly Sloppy Joe's Bar — frequented regularly by Ernest Hemingway

to Miami, settlement, a wave of immigration to the state and tourism began, reaching new records each year. Since this time, Miami has been considered the gateway to the Florida Keys and the front yard to the Everglades. As a city of immigration, Florida has long since replaced New York in its rank as number one. This is especially true for Cubans living in exile, many of who hope to return to the island of Cuba in the near future and in the meantime have made Miami into their "Little Havana."

Miami and Miami Beach are, for most tourists, synonyms for one in the same city; however, these two cities are quite different from one another. In the city of Miami, many important economic sectors have put down roots, while in the approximately 6 mile long island of Miami Beach is completely dependent on tourism. This city between the Atlantic and Biscayne Bay looks like one gigantic hotel complex, which can accommodate three times the city's actual population.

Miami / Sights

Art Deco District, The Art Deco District in the southern portion of Miami Beach dates back to the construction boom of the "golden twenties." It is presently the largest architectural museum for this style on the globe. In this historical district, there are around 800 buildings between 6th and 23rd Streets.

Tours are offered Saturdays at 10:30 am from the Ocean Front Departments, 1236 Ocean Front Drive in Miami Beach. Fee: $5; Information: Tel: (305) 672-2014.

Bass Museum of Art, 2121 Park Avenue; a renowned art museum with painting by European artists from the 14th to 20th centuries. Open from Tuesday to Saturday from 10 am to 5 pm, Sundays 1 to 5 pm; admission: $3. Tel: (305) 673-7530.

Fairchild Tropical Garden, 10901 Old Cutler Road in Coral Gables. This botanical garden with a rain forest, rare tropical plants, and over 300 species of palm trees is the largest and probably most impressive park of its kind in the United States. Open daily from 9:30 am to 4:30 pm; admission: $4 for adults, children under 12 free of charge. Information: Tel: (305) 667-1651.

Little Havana, between Southwest Eighth Street and Coral Gables. A stroll through this Cuban district is especially interesting around "Calle Ocho," leaving a great deal of impressions of the Cuban people, architecture, markets, shops and restaurants. Information: Tel: (305) 545-5643.

Metro-Dade Cultural Center, 101 West Flagler Street. This architecturally interesting and ultra-modern cultural center includes a massive library (Tel: (305) 375-2625), a Center for the Fine Arts (Tel: (305) 375-1700), and the Historical

Museum of Southern Florida (Tel: (305) 375-1492). Combined admission for the Center for Fine Arts and the Historical Museum is $8, children from 6 to 12 years of age $3. Separately: Center for the Fine Arts is $5 for adults, $2 for children from 6 to 12 years of age; Historical Museum is $4 for adults and $2 for children from 6 to 12 years of age. Admission to the library is free of charge.

Metrozoo, 12400 Southwest 152nd Street. More than 100 different species live on zoologically laid out island separated from visitors only by trenches filled with water. The animals are offered the most natural environment possible. Open daily from 10 am to 5:30 pm; admission: $8.25 for adults, $4.25 for children from 3 to 12 years of age. Information: Tel: (305) 251-0401 or (305) 251-0403.

Miami Seaquarium, 4400 Rickenbacker Causeway. In four large pools surrounded by spectator stands, a fantastic aquatic spectacle is performed. The stars are Flipper the dolphin television star and the killer whale Lolita weighing over five tons. A highlight is when Lolita balances her trainer on the tip of her snout. Open daily from 9:30 am to 6:30 pm; admission: $14.95 for adults and $10.95 for children from 3 to 12 years of age. One should plan to spend a minimum of four hours at the Miami Seaquarium. Information: Tel: (305) 361-5705.

Miccosukee Indian Village, approximately 35 miles from Miami on Tamiami Trail (US 41). Tours are offered through this authentically laid out Indian village in which alligator wrestling is performed and Indian handicrafts are sold. Propeller boat tours through the Everglades are also offered, departing from this village. Open daily from 9 am to 5 pm; admission: $5 for adults, $3.50 for children from 5 to 12 years of age. Propeller boat tours: $5 for 15 minutes, $6 for 30 minutes. Information: Tel: (305) 223-8380 and (305) 223-8388.

Monkey Jungle, 14805 Southwest 216th Street. In this lush rain forest, visitors walk along caged-in pathways while the residents of this jungle — the apes and monkeys — are free to move about in their natural environment. In a special complex, the "ape theater," performances take place every hour. Open daily from 9 am to 5 pm; admission: $9.85 for adults and $5.35 for children from 4 to 12 years of age. Information: Tel: (305) 235-1611.

Orchid Jungle, 26715 Southwest 157th Avenue. Plant and flower lovers can stroll through this park, marvelling at the rare and extraordinary orchid specimens. Open daily from 8:30 am to 5:30 pm; admission: $5 for adults, $4 for visitors from 13 to 15 years of age, $1.50 for children from 6 to 12 years of age. Information: Tel: (305) 247-4824.

Parrot Jungle, 11000 Southwest 57th Avenue. A visit to Parrot Jungle is not only worthwhile because of the numerous colourful parrots which also display their skills during performances, but it is also interesting for its beautiful park grounds including rare tropical plants and a flamingo lake. Open daily from 9:30 am to 4 pm; admission: $10 for adults, $5 for children from 3 to 12 years of age. Information: Tel: (305) 666-7834.

Planet Ocean, 3979 Rickenbacker Causeway. Here, the visitor will find a comprehensive and extensive oceanographic exhibition with scientific sophistication; however it is also made understandable for everyone. Admission: $8.50 for adults, $4 for children from 6 to 12 years of age. Information: Tel: (305) 361-5786 or (305) 361-9455.

Vizcaya Villa and Gardens, 3251 South Miami Avenue. This 70 room palace built in Italian architecture with a strictly laid out Renaissance garden was built by James Deering during a period of seven years. The park grounds are embellished with lakes and ponds, fountains, a yacht harbour as well as sculptures from Italy and France. Open daily from 9:30 am to 4:30 pm; one should allow two to three hours for a visit to the Vizcaya Villa. Admission: $8 for adults, $4 for students and visitors from 6 to 18 years of age. Information: Tel: (305) 579-2813 and (305) 579-2708.

Miami / Practical Information

Accommodation

Camping: Miami North KOA, 230 tent and RV sites, swimming pool, $21 to $27 for two persons, additional person $3 to $4, 14075 Biscayne Boulevard, reservations are recommended; Tel: (305) 940-4141 or 1-800-KOA-8818.

Miami South KOA, 288 tent and RV sites, swimming pool, $20 to $27 for two persons, additional person $3 to $6, 20675 Southwest 162nd Avenue, reservations are recommended; Tel: (305) 233-5300.

Kobe Trailer Park, 62 tent and RV sites, from $20, 11900 Northeast 16th Avenue in North Miami, reservations are recommended; Tel: (305) 893-5121.

Hotels/Motels: Alamo Hotel Apartments, 4121 Indian Creek Drive in Miami Beach, $45 for one and two persons, reservations are recommended; Tel: (305) 531-8462.

Braodmoor on the Beach Hotel, 7450 Ocean Terrace in Miami Beach, $45 to $100 for one and two persons, reservations are recommended; Tel: (305) 866-1631.

Everglades Hotel, 244 Biscayne Boulevard, $80 for one and two persons, reservations are recommended; Tel: (305) 379-5461.

Gold Dust Motel, 770 Biscayne Boulevard, $50 to $70 for one and two persons, additional person $6, reservations are recommended; Tel: (305) 757-8451.

MIAMI

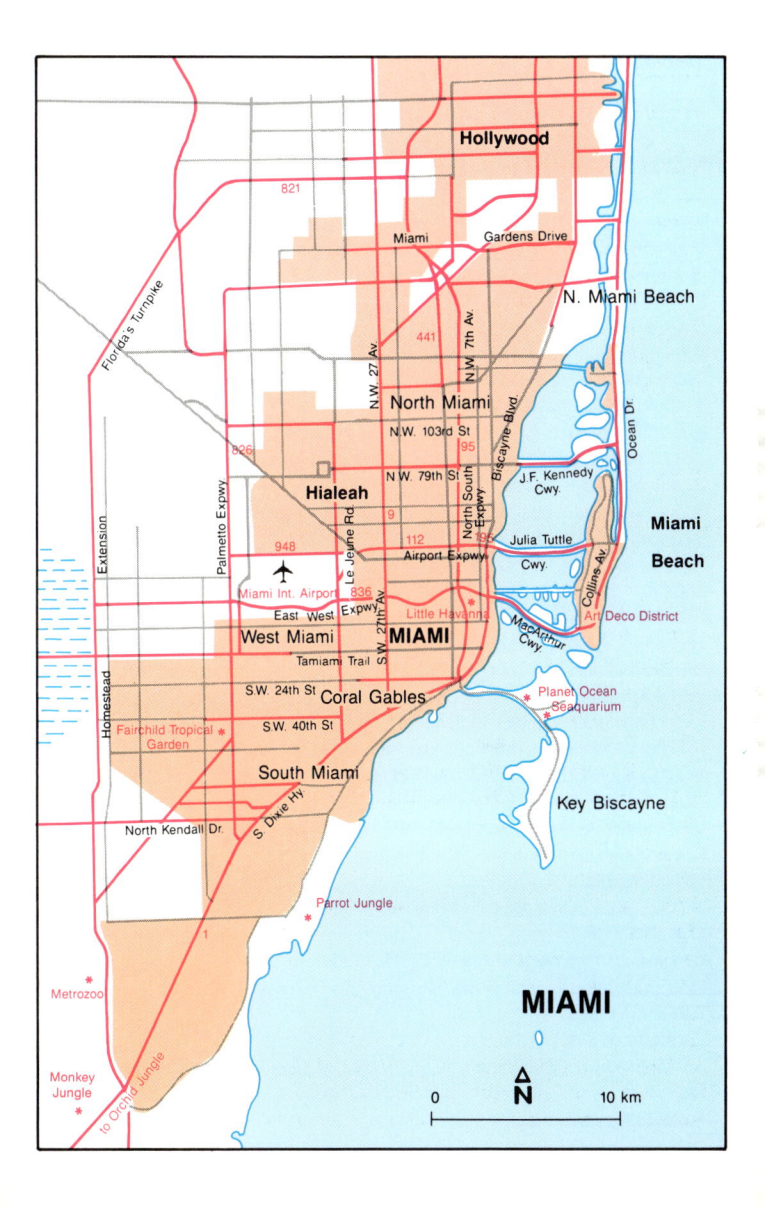

- Hollywood
- Miami Gardens Drive
- N. Miami Beach
- N.W. 7th Av.
- 441
- N.W. 27 Av.
- North Miami
- N.W. 103rd St
- 95
- Biscayne Blvd
- N.W. 79th St
- J.F. Kennedy Cwy.
- Hialeah
- 9
- 112
- North South Expwy
- Julia Tuttle Cwy.
- Airport Expwy
- Ocean Dr.
- Miami Beach
- Collins Av.
- Le Jeune Rd
- 948
- Miami Int. Airport
- 836
- East West Expwy
- S.W. 27th Av.
- Little Havana
- MIAMI
- Art Deco District
- MacArthur Cwy.
- West Miami
- Tamiami Trail
- S.W. 24th St
- Coral Gables
- Planet Ocean Seaquarium
- S.W. 40th St
- Fairchild Tropical Garden
- South Miami
- Key Biscayne
- S. Dixie Hy
- North Kendall Dr.
- Homestead
- Parrot Jungle
- 1
- Metrozoo
- Monkey Jungle
- to Orchid Jungle
- Florida's Turnpike
- 821
- Extension
- Palmetto Expwy
- 826

N

0   10 km

Hampton Inn — Miami Airport, 5125 Northwest 36th Street from $50 for one and two persons, reservations are recommended; Tel: (305) 887-2153.

Holiday Inn North Miami Golden Glades, 148 Northwest 167th Street, $70 to $90 for one and two persons, reservations are recommended; Tel: (305) 949-1441.

Ocean Roc Resort, 19505 Collins Avenue in Miami Beach, from $60 for one and two persons, additional person $8, reservations are recommended; Tel: (305) 931-7600.

Plaza Venetia, 555 Northeast 15th Street, $60 to $100 for one and two persons, reservations are recommended; Tel: (305) 374-2900.

Youth Hostels: Clay Hotel — South Miami Beach Youth Hostel, 1438 Washington Avenue, $8 for members; Tel: (305) 534-2988.

Haddon Hall Hotel — Youth Hostel SA, 1500 Collins Avenue in Miami Beach, $22 to $32 for one and two persons; Tel: (305) 531-1251.

Beaches: The Crandon Park Beach in the northern portion of Key Biscayne is over two and a half miles long with scattered palm trees. It is considered the most beautiful in Miami. Admission: $1 per vehicle; Tel: (305) 361-5421. Another beach is located in Bill Baggs Florida State Recreation Area on the southern tip of Key Biscayne. Admission: 50 cents; parking: $1; Tel: (305) 361-5811.

Remaining to be mentioned is the entire Atlantic front of Miami Beach.

Car Rental: All of the larger rental agencies have offices at the airport, in downtown Miami and in Miami Beach. Local agencies sometimes charge lower rates. Comparing prices is definitely worthwhile.

RV and Motor Home Rental: Cruise America/Motorhome Rental & Sales, 5959 Blue Lagoon Drive, 250, Miami, Florida 33126; Tel: (305) 262-9611.

Cruise America Motorhome & Van Rental & Sales, 7740 Northwest 34th Street, Miami, Florida 33122; Tel: (305) 591-7511.

Motorhomes by Maker, 17750 Cleveland Avenue, Miami, Florida 33157; Tel: (305) 235-8542.

U-Haul Main Office, 5341 Northwest 7th Avenue, Miami, Florida 33127; Tel: (305) 758-4057.

Distances: From Miami to:

Daytona Beach — 252 miles

Fort Lauderdale — 22 miles

Fort Myers — 142 miles

Jacksonville — 338 miles

Key West — 156 miles

Orlando — 228 miles

Pensacola — 649 miles
Tallahassee — 463 miles
Tampa — 245 miles
West Palm Beach — 64 miles

Medical Care: Should one encounter health problems, the following telephone numbers will be of assistance: Dade County Medical Association — Tel: (305) 324-8717 and Dade County Osteopathic Medical Association — Tel: (305) 624-9795.

Night Life and Entertainment

Most of the larger hotels offer live entertainment or shows, sometimes performances are two times per evening. The majority of night clubs are located on Northeast 79th Street and on Biscayne Boulevard. Information on current programmes and special events can be found in the daily newspapers "Miami Herald," "Miami News" and "Miami Beach Sun." Specialising on information on special events etc. is the "Miami Magazine." Information on programmes and performances in the nightclubs can be found in "This Week in Miami-Miami Beach," a brochure which is usually available free of charge in hotels, motels and newsstands.

Coconut Grove Playhouse, 3500 Main Highway, municipal stage; Tel: (305) 442-4000.

Flamenco, 991 Northeast 79th Street, two shows per evening; Tel: (305) 751-8631.

Dade County Auditorium, 2901 West Flagler Street, very popular theater; Tel: (305) 547-5414.

Monty Trainer's Dockside Raw Bar, Coconut Grove; Tel: (305) 858-1431.

Fontainebleau Hilton, 441 Collins Avenue, Grotto Bar, and La Ronde Showroom; Tel: (305) 538-2000.

Les Violins, 1751 Biscayne Boulevard, Cuban shows; Tel: (305) 371-8668.

Restaurants

Benihana of Tokyo, 1665 Northeast 79th Street Causeway, good Japanese restaurant, reservations are recommended; Tel: (305) 866-2768.

Canton of Westchester, 2501 Southwest 87th Avenue, inexpensive; Tel: (305) 552-5292.

Centro Vasco, 2235 Southwest 8th Street, specialising in Cuban cuisine; Tel: (305) 643-9606.

D'Pizza of U. M., 1118 South Dixie Highway in Coral Gables, speciality: Italian fish soup; Tel: (305) 666-5841.

Granada Restaurant, 1446 Washington Avenue in Miami Beach; Tel: (305) 534-9922.

Joe's Stone Crab, 227 Biscayne Street in Miami Beach, specialising in stone crabs; Tel: (305) 673-0365.

Old Key West Fishing Village, 18288 Collins Avenue in Miami Beach, specialising in fish and seafood, nice atmosphere.

Shopping: Miami is a hub for tourism. There are naturally also an according number of shops in which visitors can find just about everything. A selection of the larger shopping centers:

Mayfair Shopping Center, 3390 Mary Street in Coconut Grove.

Omni International Mall, Northeast 15th Street and Biscayne Boulevard.

Dadeland Mall, US 1 and State Road 826 in South Miami.

Lincoln Road Mall, South Miami near 16th Street.

Bayside Marketplace, 401 Biscayne Boulevard. Open Mondays to Fridays from 11 am to 11 pm, Saturdays from 10 am to 11 pm, Sundays from 10 am to 8 pm. This shopping center is also considered one of Miami's newest attractions; Tel: (305) 577-3344.

Cauley Square Village Shops, 22400 Old Dixie Highway. Open Monday to Saturday from 10 am to 4:30 pm; Tel: (305) 258-3543 or (305)258-0011.

There is only one supermarket open during weekends on Key Biscayne. This is located on the corner of Eastwood and Crandon Boulevard.

On Saturdays and Sundays a flea market takes place on the grounds of the Tropicaire drive-in cinema at 7751 Bird Road.

Sightseeing

Bus: A-1 Bus Lines, Inc., 1642 Northwest 21st Terrace, Miami, Florida 33142; Tel: (305) 325-1000.

All Florida Adventure Tours, 11137 North Kendall Drive, D105, Miami, Florida 33176; Tel: (305) 270-0219.

Ambassador Limousine, Inc., 19735 Northeast 36th Court, North Miami Beach, Florida 33180; Tel: (305) 931-3111.

American Sightseeing Tours, Inc., 11077 Northwest 36th Avenue, Miami, Florida 33167; Tel: (305) 688-7700.

Creative Charters, Biltmore Executive Center, 1200 Anastasia Avenue, Coral Gables, Florida 33134; Tel: (305) 445-7318 or (305) 446-6614.

Greyhound Travel Service, 99 Northeast 4th Street, Miami, Florida 33132; Tel: (305) 358-4208.

Red Top Sedan Service, 11077 Northwest 36th Avenue, Miami, Florida 33167; Tel: (305) 688-7700.

What would Miami be without its famous Art Deco district ▶

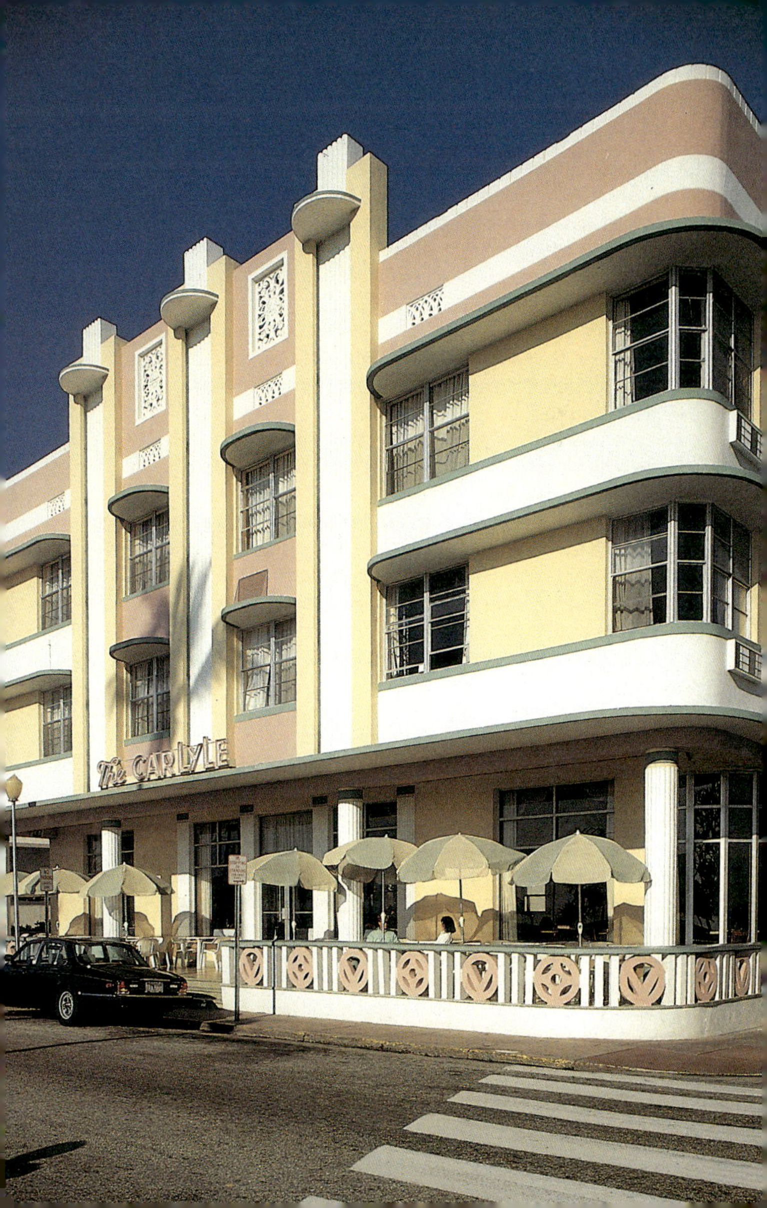
The CARLYLE

Helicopters: Miami Helicopter Service, 1050 MacArthur Causeway; Tel: (305) 377-0934.

Gold Coast Helicopter, 15101 Biscayne Boulevard; Tel: (305) 940-1009.

Dade Helicopter Jet Service; Tel: (305) 374-3737.

Ships: With the paddlewheel steamer "Island Queen," visitors can get to know Biscayne Bay during a two-hour tour.

Northeast 5th Street and Biscayne Boulevard; Tel: (305) 370-5119.

Sea Escape sets off daily (except Fridays) on a one-day tour to Freeport in the Bahamas. The price is $99; departures 8:30 am, return at 11pm. Information: 1080 Port Boulevard; Tel: (305) 379-0000.

Nikko Gold Coast Cruises, 10800 Collins Avenue, Miami Beach; Tel: (305) 945-5461.

Tiger's Airboat Tours, $7 for adults, $4 for children from 4 to 12 years of age, 8918 Southwest 150 North Court Circle; Tel: (305) 559-5250.

Sports and Recreation

Miami by Bicycle: The city has an extensive network of bicycle paths making it well suited to cycling. There are also shops which rent out bicycles. Exact addresses and telephone numbers can be found in the local yellow pages. Information and the brochure "Miami on Two Wheels a Day" is available through the Metro-Dade Department of Tourism, 234 West Flagler Street. Information is also available through the Dade County Parks Department; Tel: (305) 579-2676.

Dog Races: Biscayne Dog Track, 320 Northwest 115th Street.

Flagler Dog Track, 401 Northwest 38th Court.

Jai Alai: Miami Jai-Alai, 3500 Northwest 37th Avenue.

Horse Races: Calder Race Course, 21001 Northwest 27th Avenue.

Tennis and Golf: Public tennis courts can be found in Flamingo Park, 1000 12th Street; in Miami Beach and on Key Biscayne. In addition, there are also several public golf courses. Further information: Tel: (305) 579-2676.

Transportation

Trains: The Amtrak Station is located at 8303 Northwest 37th Avenue; Tel: (305) 691-0125.

Buses: The public bus system is operated by the Metropolitan Transport Authority, 3300 Northwest 32nd Avenue. Available here free of charge are bus schedules and route maps. Fares: $1; transfers: 25 cents.

On the route from West 21st Street in Hialeah via downtown to Kendall Drive, there is a modern transit system with an elevated railway. It is planned to expand this "Metrorail." Fares: $1; Information: Tel: (305) 638-6700.

Greyhound Terminals in: Hialeah, 93 West Okeechobee Road; Coral Gables, 2300 Salzedo Avenue; Miami Beach, 7101 Harding Avenue; in the northern portion of Miami Beach, 16250 Biscayne Boulevard.

Trailways Terminal: 99 Northeast 4th Street.

Air Travel: The Miami International Airport (MIA), is located approximately 5 miles from downtown Miami on Le Jeune Road and Northwest 36th Street. It is one of the largest airports in the world. Information: Tel: (305) 871-7090.

Shuttle Service from the Airport: Supershuttle, 4300 Northwest 14th Street, Miami; Tel: (305) 871-8210.

Orientation: Flagler Street running east to west and Miami Avenue running north to south meet in the center of Miami and divide the city into four sectors: northwest, northeast, southwest and southeast. Street numbers begin from this intersection. The larger the number, the further one is from the center of the city. Avenues, courts and places run north and south; streets, lanes and terraces, from east to west.

Taxi: Miami's taxi fares range around $1.20 per mile and 20 cents per minute for waiting time.

Important Addresses

Greater Miami Chamber of Commerce, 1601 Biscayne Boulevard, Miami, Florida 33145; Tel: (305) 350-7700.

Greater Miami Convention and Visitors Bureau, 701 Brickell Avenue, Suite 2700, Miami, Florida 33131; Tel: (305) 539-3000.

Greater Miami Hotel and Motel Association, Inc., 300 Biscayne Boulevard Way, Suite 719, Miami, Florida 33131; Tel: (305) 371-2030.

Miami Beach Chamber of Commerce, 1920 Meridian Avenue, Miami Beach, Florida 33139; Tel: (305) 672-1270.

Miami Beach Resort Hotel Association, 407 Lincoln Road, Miami Beach, Florida 33139; Tel: (305) 531-3553.

Miami Convention Center, 400 Southeast 2nd Avenue, Miami, Florida 33131; Tel: (305) 579-6341.

Money

Many foreign visitors find the US dollars confusing because they are all similar in size and colour, the difference only apparent in the printed value and which portrait appears on the front. Those visiting Florida from foreign countries should exchange money into dollars before leaving since some banks will not exchange foreign currencies, or one must order foreign currencies in advance if changing dollars back.

Traveller's cheques are accepted almost everywhere as cash. Therefore, it is a good idea to bring most of one's travel budget in traveller's cheques since they can be replaced if lost or stolen.

Credit cards are also widely accepted and almost a necessity if planning to rent a car. A credit card will also prove handy if one unexpectedly needs to pay larger sums for medical care. Visa and Mastercard (Eurocard/Access) are more widely accepted than American Express and they are accepted in most banks, whereas for American Express, one must go specifically to an American Express office, which might not always be conveniently located.

Motorway Tolls

In Florida, there are a few roadways charging tolls from 20 cents to $1. This is either paid at the toll stations or by tossing change into the receptacles at the entrances to the roads. Roads and bridges charging toll are:
- In Jacksonville, the Hart, Mathews, Trout River and Fuller Warren Bridges,
- The State Road 115 to Jacksonville, the J. Turner Butler Expressway,
- From Orlando to J. F. Kennedy Space Center, the Bee Line Expressway/Highway 528,
- In the commercial district south of Orlando, the Holland East-West Expressway,
- In Tampa, the South Crosstown Expressway,
- From St. Petersburg to St. Petersburg Beach, the Pinellas Bayway,
- From Naples to Andytown, the Everglades Parkway/Alligator Alley,
- From Wildwood to Homestead, the Florida Turnpike/Sunshine Parkway,
- From downtown Miami to the airport, the Airport Expressway,
- From downtown Miami to the Palmetto Expressway, the East-West Expressway/Highway 836.

These routes are the quickest in reaching the given destinations. Alternate routes also exist.

Nature Reserves

Nature reserves, especially the national and state parks, are among the main tourist attractions in the United States. This is, however, not as much the case in the State of Florida as it is, for example, in the western portions of the United States. Still they count among the attractions of Florida alongside the fantastic

---

Parrot Jungle in Miami — amid the lush subtropical vegetation, parrots perform their antics ▶

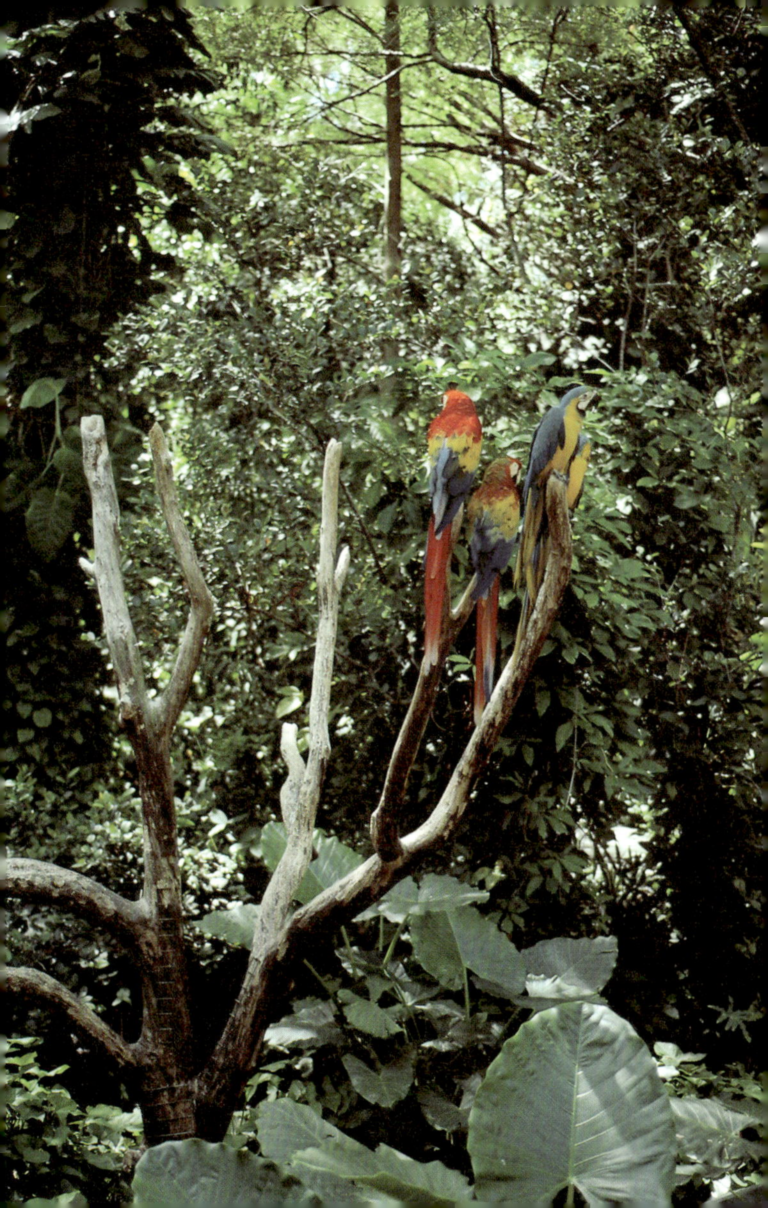

Nature Reserves

beaches and of course the colossal amusement parks. In total, there are seven national parks and 105 state parks in Florida.

The national parks are administrated by the National Park Service, a division of the Ministry of the Interior. The smaller and often just as beautiful state parks fall under the administration of the individual states.

Within the national parks, any private use or change in the natural condition of the park is prohibited. This includes any construction for commercial purposes other than those covered by the concessions awarded by the National Park Service in regard to forestry, hunting, water rights etc. Even airlines are not permitted to fly over national parks.

Due to these strict regulations which protect these areas, the wildlife is very trusting, not having learned to fear humans. Animals quite often approach visitors without any shyness.

The parks are not fenced in; thus, the freedom of movement of the wildlife is not restricted in any way. The only noticeable borders are marked by signs along the roadways at the entrances to the parks.

At the booths at the entrances to the parks, an admission fee of $5 per vehicle is charged, or, if entering on foot or by bus, a fee of $1 to $2 per person is charged. Those who plan to visit at least five of these parks should buy the "Golden Eagle Passport" for $25 which is valid for all of the parks belonging to the National Park System for one year. Seniors can obtain the "Golden Age Passport" which is valid for free admission to all of the parks and includes reduced rates at the campsites run by the parks. These passports are available at the entrances to the national parks or by contacting the following address: United States Department of the Interior, National Park Service, P.O. Box 37127, Washington, DC 20013-7127.

At the most beautiful and interesting points, there are usually signs with the most important information.

The friendly park rangers in the brown uniforms are employees of the federal government, and view themselves not only as protectors of nature but are also willing to answer any questions and help visitors in any way they can. At certain times posted in the visitor centers or at the campsites, a diverse programme is offered free of charge. These ranger-led activities range from slide shows and films to lectures at sites of natural interest or an evening bonfire lasting several hours to informative hikes.

The National Park Service also operates the visitor centers, in which excellent informational material and hiking maps are available. These visitor centers are usually equipped with a lounge, a lecture hall for lectures and slide shows, an information desk and an exhibition room.

Practical Information

Information on campsite capacity and vacancies is often posted at the entrances to the parks.

Lodges, cottages, cabins, souvenir shops, and tour organisers in the parks are operated on a concession basis. Depending on level of comfort, furnishing and the national park, one must expect to pay around $20 to $50 per night for one or two persons in accommodations.

Informational material on national parks can be obtained by contacting: Public Information Officer, National Park Service, US Department of the Interior, 1100 Ohio Drive Southwest, Washington DC 20242, or directly from the individual parks. The addresses for these are listed under the appropriate entries.

Orlando

Population: 130,000

Orlando, in the heart of central Florida is considered the Mecca for amusement park tourists and the entertainment center of Florida. The superlative world of Mickey Mouse alone can boast about two million visitors per year. Thus, it is not surprising that the cypress swamps surrounding Orlando have long since been replaced with highways, making Orlando a transportation hub of the state of Florida. The most important approaches by car are Interstate 4, which connects Daytona Beach on the east coast with Tampa on the Gulf of Mexico, and the Florida Turnpike, a heavily travelled north-south route in Florida.

Modern architecture amid an expansive and diverse landscape is one facet of Orlando. Within the city limits are no less than 47 parks with a total of 54 lakes. Of these parks, the following are especially worth visiting: Eola Park, East Central Avenue; Leu Gardens, 1730 North Forest Avenue; Tel: (407) 894-6021 as well as the Loch Haven Park, Princeton Boulevard and Mills Avenue. Located in the latter are the two Museums John Young Science Center, 810 East Rollins Street; Tel: (407) 896-7151, and the Loch Haven Art Center, 2461 North Mills Avenue; Tel: (407) 896-4231.

Orlando / Sights

Boardwalk and Baseball, on Interstate 4 and US 27. This is a newer amusement park with various shows, numerous attraction and a very fast roller coaster and an IMAX theater with a six story screen (at present showing a film about the Grand Canyon). Open Sundays to Fridays from am to 6 pm, Saturdays

Orlando

from 9 am to 9 pm. Admission: $19 for adults, $15 for children with a height of up to 48 inches; Tel: (813) 424-2424.

Church Street Station, 129 West Church Street. In this district are beautifully restored Victorian houses from the period around the latter 19th century. Antiques shops and shops offering souvenirs as well as restaurants and saloons offering entertainment — and all of this in the style of this bygone era. Open daily from 11 am to 2 am. Admission: $15 for adults, $10 for children from 3 to 12 years of age; Tel: (407) 422-4234.

Citrus Tower, on US 27 near Clermont. On a 210 foot high platform, one stands on the highest observation platform in Florida. From this vantage point, there is a magnificent view of the citrus producing regions of central Florida. Open daily from 8 am to 6 pm; admission: $3 for adults; $2 for visitors between the ages of 10 and 15, children under 10 free of charge; Tel: (904) 394-8585.

Cypress Gardens →*Winter Haven*

Disney World →*Walt Disney World Resort*

Gatorland Zoo, approximately 4 miles north of Kissimmee on the US 441, 14501 South Orange Blossom Trail. Living in this landscape of swamps and lagoons are more than 5,000 alligators and crocodiles. One can wander through the grounds on boardwalks or ride the Gatorland Zoo Express. Especially popular is the "Gator Jumparoo Show." From April to September open daily from 8 am to 8 pm; October to March daily from 8 am to 6 pm. Admission: $8.95 for adults and $5.95 for children from 3 to 11 years of age; Tel: (407) 855-5496.

Sea World, 7007 Sea World Drive near the exit from the Bee Line Expressway onto Interstate 4. Among the diverse and interesting attractions in this 138 acre park are the shows "The Legend of Shamu," "USO Water Ski Show," "Window to the Sea," "New Friends" and "Sea Lions of the Silver Screen " with trained dolphins and the killer whale Shamu, seals, walruses and otters. In addition, there is a huge shark pool with a window for underwater observation. Also offered here are an entertaining acrobatic water ski show, a Japanese village, in which pearl divers demonstrate their work, the multi-media show "Undersea Fantasy" and botanical gardens. For Sea World, one should plan an entire day into the travel itinerary. Admission: $26.95 for adults, $22.95 for children from 3 to 9 years of age; Tel: (407) 351-3600 or 1-800-432-1178 within Florida.

Universal Studios Florida, 1000 Universal Studios Plaza, Orlando. In the spring of 1990, Universal Studios opened another extensive amusement park built

---

What was earlier a swamp region is now a vibrant city: with the completion of Flagler's East Coast Railroad, Miami experienced a boom ▶

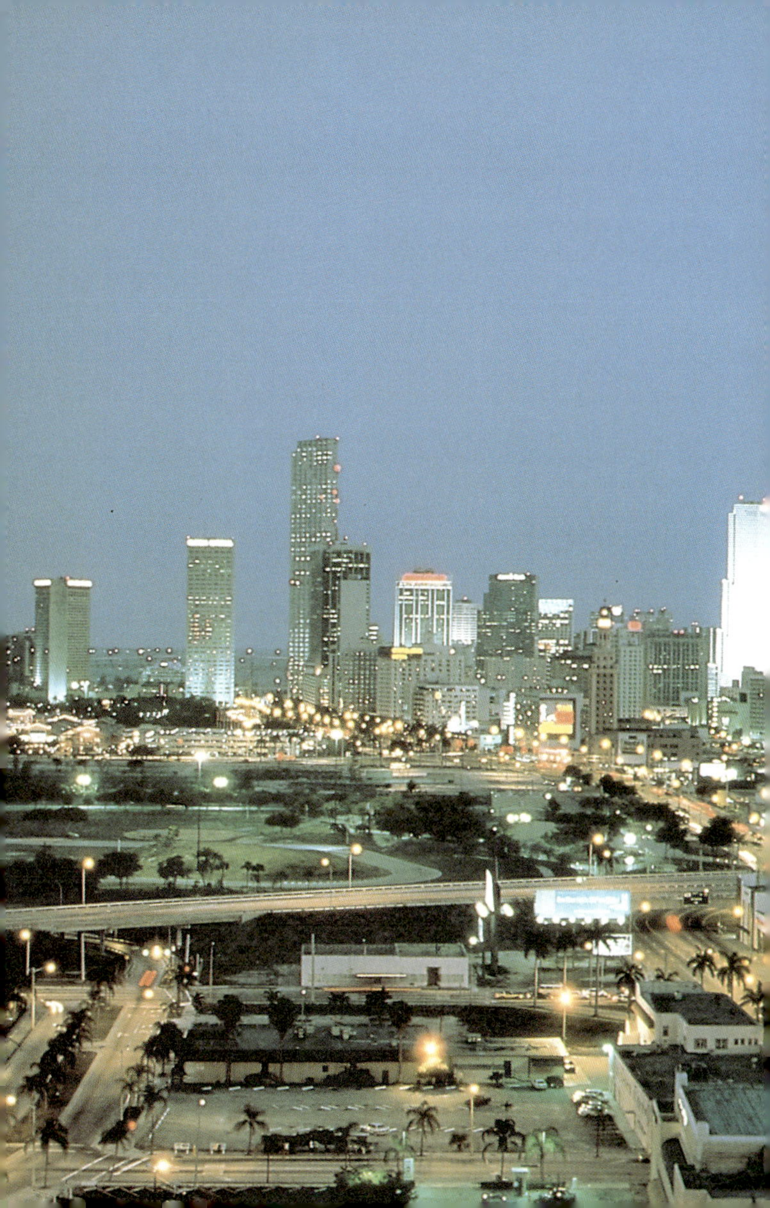

after the prototype in Los Angeles, California. Visitors can experience the lively atmosphere of the studios to find himself in perfectly replicated scenes from the most famous Hollywood films like "E.T.," "King Kong" and "Back to the Future." Admission is $31 for adults and $25 for children from 3 to 9 years of age; Tel: (407) 363-8000.

Wet'n Wild, 6200 International Drive in Orlando. This is one of the largest aquatic amusement parks in the world. Imaginative water slides are twisted into the most diverse shapes, some of which require a good deal of courage. This park is open from mid February to December, depending on the season from 9 am to 9pm. Admission: $18.95 for adults, $16.95 for children from 3 to 12 years of age; Tel: (407) 351-1800 or (407) 351-3200.

Orlando / Practical Information

Accommodation

Camping: Best Holiday Trav-L-Park, 254 tent and RV sites, from $22 for two persons, additional person $2, swimming pool, 1600 West 33rd Street; Tel: (407) 648-5441 or 1-800-323-8899.

Lake Breeze Park, 64 tent and RV sites, from $22 for two persons, additional person $2 to $3, reservations are recommended, 2040 Lee Road; Tel: (407) 293-9391.

Orlando/Winter Garden Campground, 380 tent and RV sites, 2 heated swimming pools, from $20 for two persons, additional person $2, reservations are recommended, 279 West Highway 50; Tel: (407) 656-1415.

Walt Disney World/Orlando Southeast KOA, 144 tent and RV sites, lakeside, $16 to $22 for two persons, additional person $2, reservations are recommended, 12343 Narcoosee Road; Tel: (407) 277-5075 or 1-800-999-KAMP.

Yogi Bear's Jellystone Park Camp, 550 tent and RV sites, $18 for two persons, additional person $2, 2 lakes, bathing facilities, 9200 Turkey Lane Road; Tel: (407) 351-4394.

Hotels/Motels: American Motor Inn, 11639 East Colonial Drive, $34 to $45 for one and two persons, additional person $3; Tel: (407) 282-0494.

Comfort Inn Downtown, 720 South Orange Blossom Trail, $35 to $55 for one and two persons (depending on the season), additional person $6; Tel: (407) 841-0788.

Comfort Inn International, 5825 International Drive, $35 to $55 for one and two persons (depending on the season), additional person $5; Tel: (407) 351-4100.

Days Inn Airport, 2323 McCoy Road, $35 to $60 for one and two persons, additional person $6, free shuttle service to and from the airport; Tel: (407) 859-6100.

Days Inn Midtown, 3300 South Orange Blossom Trail, $30 to $45 for one and two persons, additional person $6; Tel: (407) 422-4521.

Days Inn Orlando, 2500 West 33rd Street, $30 to $65 for one and two persons, additional person $6; Tel: (407) 841-3731.

Delta Hotel, 6301 International Drive, $35 to $45 for one and two persons (depending on the season); Tel: (407) 351-4430.

International Inn, 6327 International Drive, $35 to $45 for one and two persons; Tel: (407) 351-4444.

Youth Hostels: International Hostel, 420 Highland Avenue, $8 for members; Tel: (407) 841-8867.

Young Women's Community Club, 107 East Hillcrest Street, restricted to women between the ages of 17 and 37, $8; Tel: (407) 425-2502.

Vehicle Rental

Cars: In addition to the larger rental agencies, there are a large number of less expensive local rental agencies. These can be found in the local yellow pages.

RV and Motor Home Rental: Cruise America, 5301 McCoy Road, Orlando, Florida 32812; Tel: (407) 857-8282.

Holiday RV Rental Leasing, Inc., 5001 Sand Lake Road, Orlando, Florida 32819; Tel: (407) 351-8888.

Medical Care

First Aid Medical Center, 7411 International Drive, Orlando; Tel: (407) 351-6063.

Florida Hospital, 601 East Rollins Street, Orlando; Tel: (407) 897-1029.

Night Life and Entertainment

Bavarian Bierhaus, 7430 Republic Drive, Bavarian entertainment, beer, food and music; Tel: (407) 351.0191.

King Henry's Feast, 8984 International Drive, non-stop entertainment programme with sword fights, a comedy show and magicians etc. Includes a banquet. All-inclusive price of $26.95 for adults and $18.95 for children from 3 to 11 years of age, reservations are recommended; Tel: (407) 351-5151.

Mardi Gras — at Mercado Festival Center, offers a two-hour comedy show also with Dixieland jazz. A four course meal is included in the price of $27.95 for adults and $19.95, reservations are recommended; Tel: (407) 351-5151.

Restaurants: Bavarian Schnitzel House, 6159 Westwood Boulevard, medium price category with entertainment; Tel: (407) 352-8484.

Orlando

Bay Street Restaurant, 6115 Westwood Boulevard, medium price category; Tel: (407) 352-9419.

Charlie's Lobster House, 3415 Aloma Avenue in Winter Park, specialising in fish and seafood, reservations are recommended; Tel: (407) 677-7352.

Ming Garden, 6432 International Drive, good Chinese restaurant, medium price category; Tel: (407) 352-8044.

Ran-Getsu of Tokyo, 8400 International Drive, medium price category; Tel: (407) 345-0044.

Shopping: In this city dominated by tourists, there are an accordingly high proportion of imaginative and interesting shopping opportunities, for example: A-International Fruit Basket, 1718 North Goldenroad; Tel: (407) 277-0489.

Flea World, 610 North Orange Avenue; Tel: (407) 841-1792.

Florida Mall, 8001 South Orange Avenue; Tel: (407) 851-6255.

Mercado Mediterranean Village, 8445 International Drive; Tel: (407) 345-9337.

Sightseeing

One-hour tours of downtown Orlando begin every Thursday at 10 am at Wall Street Plaza. Information is available by contacting: The Downtown Development Board, 120 South Orange Avenue; Tel: (407) 425-0534 or Junior League of Orlando-Winter Park, 125 North Lucerne Circle; Tel: (407) 843-7463.

Tours of the city and especially the attractions in the surrounding regions are offered by:

American Sightseeing Tours, Inc., 9526 Boyce Avenue, Orlando, Florida 32824; Tel: (407) 859-2250.

Festival Tours, Inc., 737 West Oak Bridge Road, Orlando, Florida 32809; Tel: (407) 859-5712.

Florida Tour Lines, 4352 Southwest 34th Street, Orlando, Florida 32811; Tel: (407) 841-6400.

Grey Line of Orlando, 4590 L. B. McLeod Road, Orlando, Florida 32802; Tel: (407) 422-0744.

Greyhound Travel Services, Inc., 300 West Amelia Street, Orlando, Florida 32801; Tel: (407) 423-8186.

Mears Transportation Group, 324 West Gore Street, Orlando, Florida 32806; Tel: (407) 839-1570.

Orlando Tour Lines 2301 South Division Avenue, Orlando, Florida 32805; Tel: (407) 422-2242.

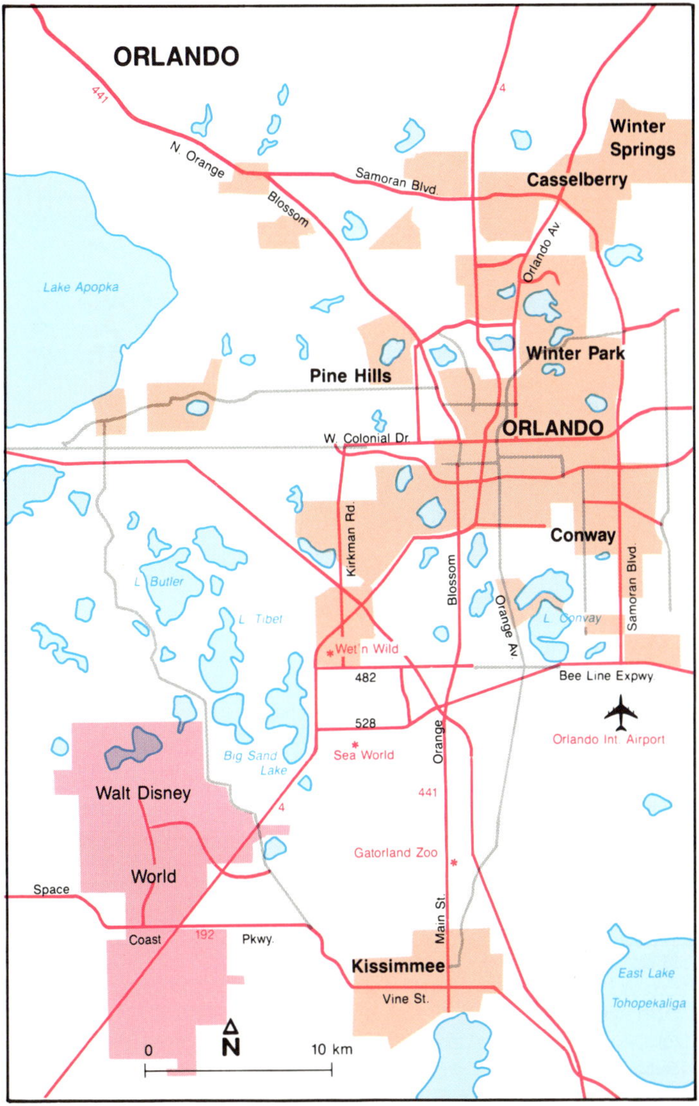

ORLANDO
441
4
Winter Springs
N. Orange
Samoran Blvd.
Casselberry
Blossom
Orlando Av.
Lake Apopka
Winter Park
Pine Hills
ORLANDO
W. Colonial Dr.
Kirkman Rd.
Conway
Blossom
Samoran Blvd.
L. Butler
L. Tibet
Orange Av.
L. Conway
Wet'n Wild
482
Bee Line Expwy.
528
Orlando Int. Airport
Big Sand Lake
Sea World
Orange
441
Walt Disney
4
Gatorland Zoo
World
Space
Main St.
Coast
192
Pkwy.
Kissimmee
East Lake Tohopekaliga
Vine St.
0
N
10 km

Sports and Recreation

Owing to the many lakes and rivers in and around Orlando, *aquatic sports* are especially popular — predominantly fishing and boating.

Tennis Courts: Exposition Park; Tel: (407) 849-2461; Sanlando Park; Tel: (407) 869-5966.

Golf Courses: at Lake Buena Vista; Tel: (407) 828-3741 and (407) 824-2200; in Orlando Dubsdred; Tel: (407) 843-7311 and in Wedgefield; Tel: (407) 568-2116.

Dog Races: Sanford-Orlando Kennel Club, Dog Track Road in Longwood; Tel: (407) 831-1600.

Super Seminole Greyhound Park, 2000 Seminola Boulevard in Casselberry; Tel: (407) 699-4510.

Jai Alai: Florida Jai Alai, Inc., 6405 South Highway in Fern Park; Tel: (407) 339-6221.

Eddie Graham Sports Stadium; Tel: (407) 282-0291.

Transportation

Trains: Amtrak Station, 1400 Sligh Boulevard; Tel: 1-800-USA-RAIL, located south of the center of town.

Buses: Greyhound Terminal, 300 West Amelia Street; Tel: (407) 843-7720. Continental Trailways, 30 North Hughey Avenue; Tel: (407) 422-7107.

Both bus terminals are located in the downtown area.

Distances from Orlando to:

John F. Kennedy Space Center — 47 miles

Daytona Beach — 54 miles

St. Augustine — 61 miles

St. Petersburg — 66 miles

Jacksonville — 135 miles

Fort Myers — 154 miles

Fort Lauderdale — 209 miles

Miami — 232 miles

Key West — 372 miles

Pensacola — 435 miles

Airport: The Orlando International Airport (MCO) is located approximately 7 miles south of the city on the Bee Line Expressway, 1 Airport Boulevard; Tel: (407) 826-2001.

Important Addresses

Orlando Chamber of Commerce, P.O. Box 1234, Orlando, Florida 32802; Tel: (407) 425-1234.

Orlando/Orange County Convention & Visitors Bureau, 7208 Sand Lake Road, Suite 300, Orlando, Florida 32819; Tel: (407) 363-5800.

Palm Beach / West Palm Beach

Total population: 70,000

In 1894, Henry Flagler established the preconditions for the development of the eastern coast of Florida with his railway, the Lake Worth, and found a section of the coastline which was covered with countless, large coconut palms. The name Palm Beach was inevitable. The smaller Palm Beach lies on a 14 mile long and a little over a half of a mile wide strip of land east of the lake and is considered the city of the wealthy. Accordingly pretentious are the villas which line Worth Avenue.

West Palm Beach, on the other side of the lake is less confined and less bound by tradition. It holds a large degree of attraction for sports and recreation.

Palm Beach / Sights

Dreher Park Zoo, 1301 Summit Boulevard. This park is not only a zoological garden but also worth seeing for the vegetation growing here. The Betty Cardinal Nature Path, for example, is lined with plant from all over the globe. Open daily from 9 am to 5 pm; admission: $4 for adults, $2 for children from 3 to 12 years of age; Tel: (407) 533-0887.

Henry Morrison Flagler Museum, Poinciana Plaza on Whitehall Way near Coconut Row. The former residence of the railway pioneer contains valuable furnishings and interesting articles from the infancy of the railway. Among these is also Flagler's private railroad car "The Rambler." Admission: $5 for adults and $2 for children from 6 to 12 years of age. Open Tuesdays to Saturdays from 10 am to 5 pm, Sundays from noon to 5 pm, closed Mondays; Tel: (407) 655-2833.

Lion Country Safari, on Southern Boulevard, 15 miles west of West Palm Beach. The tongue-in-cheek greeting at the entrance "Trespassers Will be Eaten" is certainly also a warning that visitors should not leave their vehicles. Lions, giraffes, zebras, ostriches, elephants and other animals can roam about freely in this park. In addition, boat tours, an animal clinic, elephant rides, and jungle golf as well as a dinosaur park offer a diversified palette of recreation and entertainment. One should allow four hours for a visit to Lion Country Safari. Open daily from 9:30 am to 5:30 pm; admission: $11.95 for adults and $9.95 for children from 3 to 15 years of age; Tel: (407) 793-1084.

Norton Gallery of Art, 1451 South Olive Avenue. This museum is among the most significant cultural attractions in Florida. The resident expedition is extraordinary. One should definitely allow at least an hour for a visit to this museum. Open Tuesdays to Saturdays from 10 am to 5 pm, Sundays from

1 to 5 pm, closed Mondays. Suggested admission: $3 for adults and $2 for children from 3 to 12 years of age; Tel: (407) 832-5194.

South Florida Science Museum, 1 Dreher Trail North. In addition to on-hands exhibitions in the Discovery Hall, this museum is worth visiting because of the Aldrin Planetarium and the South Florida Aquarium. One should plan on spending two to three hours for a visit to this museum. Open Tuesday to Saturday from 10 am to 5 pm, Sundays from noon to 5 pm, open longer on Fridays until 11 pm. Admission: $5 for adults, $1.50 for children from 4 to 12 years of age; Tel: (407) 832-1988.

State Park: John D. MacArthur Beach State Park, 10900 State Road 703, Singer Island, North Palm Beach, Florida 33408; Tel: (407) 627-6097.

Palm Beach / Practical Information

Accommodation

Camping: Lion Country Safari KOA, 200 tent and RV sites, $18 for three persons, additional person $2, near the Lion Country Safari Park (→*Sights, this entry*), reservations are recommended; Tel: (407) 793-9797.

Palm Beach Gardens Campground, 105 RV sites, $18 for two persons, additional person $2, 4063 Hood Road in Lake Park, reservations are recommended; Tel: (407) 622-8212.

Vacation Inn Resort, 400 RV sites, $25 for two persons, additional person $2, 6566 North Military Trail; Tel: (407) 848-6166.

Hotels/Motels: Days Inn, 2300 West 45th Street, $40 to $75 for one and two persons (depending on the season), additional person $5; Tel: (407) 689-0454.

Knights Inn, 2200 45th Street, $40 to $75 for one and two persons (depending on the season), additional person $3; Tel: (407) 478-1554.

Parkview Motor Lodge, 4710 South Dixie Highway, $40 to $80 for one and two persons (depending on the season), additional person $6, reservations are recommended; Tel: (407) 833-4644.

Restaurants: Charley's Crab, 456 South Ocean Boulevard, specialising in fish and seafood, reservations are recommended; Tel: (407) 659-1500.

Testa's Restaurant, 221 Royal Poinciana Way, specialising in steaks, seafood and Italian cuisine, reservations are recommended; Tel: (407) 832-0992.

Sightseeing

Bus: Co Tran-Palm Beach County Transit, Building S-1440, Palm Beach International Airport, West Palm Beach, Florida 33406; Tel: (407) 686-4555.

Ships: Crown Cruise Line, P.O. Box 3000, Boca Raton, Florida 33431; Tel: 1-800-841-7447.

Empress Dining Cruises, Inc., 900 East Blue Heron Boulevard, Riviera Beach, Florida 33404; Tel: (407) 842-0882.

Sports and Recreation

Dog Races: Palm Beach Kennel Club, 1111 North Congress Avenue, West Palm Beach, Florida 33409; Tel: (407) 683-2222.

Jai Alai: The Fronton, Inc., Palm Beach Jai Alai, 1415 West 45th Street, West Palm Beach, Florida 33407; Tel: (407) 844-2444.

Transportation

Distances from West Palm Beach to:

Fort Lauderdale — 44 miles

Miami — 69 miles

Fort Myers — 124 miles

John F. Kennedy Space Center — 125 miles

St. Petersburg — 127 miles

St. Augustine — 151 miles

Alligators prefer a freshwater environment in contrast to their cousins the crocodiles

Orlando — 167 miles
Daytona Beach — 189 miles
Key West — 244 miles
Jacksonville — 277 miles
Pensacola — 595 miles

Airport: Palm Beach International Airport (PBI), International Apt., Building 846, West Palm Beach, Florida 33406; Tel: (407) 471-7400.

The airport is located approximately 3 miles west of the city.

RV and Motor Home Rental: Cruise America — RV Rental, 5838 North Military Trail, West Palm Beach, Florida 33407; Tel: (407) 683-2460.

U-Haul Center of Palm Beach, 4371 Okeechobee Boulevard, West Palm Beach, Florida 33409; Tel: (407) 684-0428.

Important Addresses

Tourist Development Council, Palm Beach County, 1555 Palm Beach Lakes Boulevard, Suite 204, West Palm Beach, Florida 33401; Tel: (407) 471-3995.

Chamber of Commerce of the Palm Beaches, 401 North Flagler Drive, P.O. Box 2931, West Palm Beach, Florida 33401; Tel: (407) 833-3711.

Panama City / Panama City Beach

Population: 35,000

The city of Panama on St. Andrews Bay is approximately 104 miles east of Pensacola and is considered the entertainment center of northwestern Florida. The most activity is concentrated in Panama City Beach.

Located here are the amusement parks "Miracle Ship" and "Shipwreck Island" directly adjacent. These are a theme parks with various aquatic attractions. Interesting demonstration on how venom is gained from snakes can be seen and heard in the Snake-a-Torium.

Panama City / Practical Information

Accommodation

Camping: Panama City Beach KOA, 280 tent and RV sites, tents $14 for two persons, RV's $19 for two persons, additional person $2, 8800 Thomas Drive; Tel: (904) 234-5032.

Hotels/Motels: Econo Lodge, 11004 West Highway 98A, $35 to $60 for one and two persons (depending on the season), additional person $6; Tel: (904) 234-7334.

Holiday Lodge, 6400 West Highway 98A, $35 to $60 for one and two persons (depending on the season), additional person $3; Tel: (904) 234-2114.

Pana Roc Motel, 5507 Thomas Drive, $30 to $60 for one and two persons (depending on the season), additional person $5; Tel: (904) 234-2775.

Seascape Inn, 15505 West Highway 98A, $30 to $65 for one and two persons (depending on the season), additional person $3; Tel: (904) 234-3315.

Surf High Inn, 10611 West Highway 98A, $25 to $45 for one and two persons, additional person $3 to $5 (depending on the season); Tel: (904) 234-2129.

Youth Hostel: Sangraal by-the-Sea, 226 College Avenue, $8 for members; Tel: (904) 785-6226.

Beaches: The fantastic sand beach of Panama City Beach is one of the main attractions of this city. In addition, there is also good swimming on Shell Island. This island is also well suited for scuba diving, snorkelling or merely lying in the sun. The island is only accessible by boat. Boats for Shell Island depart from Captain Anderson's Marina, 5500 North Grand Lagoon Drive and from the Treasure Island Marina.

Museum: The Junior Museum of Bay County at 1731 Jenks Avenue is an interesting and educational museum, focussing on history. In addition there is an excellent educational trail through the swamp areas. Admission is free of charge; Tel: (904) 169-6128.

Restaurants: Of course, specialities from the sea dominate the menus in the restaurants of this city. In addition, however, there are sufficient alternatives.

In Panama City:

Aegean Restaurant, 1031 West 15th American, serving seafood and Greek cuisine, closed Sundays; Tel: (904) 769-5514.

Harbour House, 3001A West 10th Street, specialising in meat dishes and seafood; Tel: (904) 785-9053.

In Panama City Beach:

Captain Anderson's Restaurant, 5551 North Lagoon Drive, closed Sundays; Tel: (904) 234-2225.

Harold's Oyster Bar & Restaurant, 8503 Thomas Avenue; Tel: (904) 235-8952.

Treasure Ship Main Dining Room, 3605 Thomas Drive, a restaurant with a very nice atmosphere housed in a Spanish galleon; Tel: (904) 234-8881.

RV and Motor Home Rental: Northwest Campers, 4133 Highway 231, Panama City, Florida 32404; Tel: (904) 763-3945.

U-Haul Moving and Storage, 1026 West 15th Street, Panama City, Florida 32401; Tel: (904) 769-3268.

Transportation

Airport: Panama City-Bay County Regional Airport (PFN), 3173 Airport Road, Panama City, Florida 32405; Tel: (904) 763-6751.

Important Addresses
Panama City Beach Convention and Visitors Bureau, 12015 West Highway 98A, Panama City Beach, Florida 32407; Tel: (904) 233-6503.

Pensacola

Population: 58,000

Pensacola is located in the northwestern extreme of Florida and is a city with a relatively long history. For a period of around 300 years, this city was under the rule of Spain, Great Britain, France, the Confederates and finally the United States. This city experienced 13 changes in rulers, and this only since the end of the 17th century.

The history of Pensacola is especially apparent in the old district of the city. Having meanwhile gained the status of an attraction, Seville Square has beautifully renovated buildings from the 19th century in which art galleries, antiques shops, museums, restaurants and numerous shops are housed, attracting more and more visitors to this area. Some of these buildings, like the Charles Levallé House from 1810 (the oldest building in Pensacola), the Hispanic Building or the Clara Barkley Dorr House can be toured free of charge. Information: Tel: (904) 434-1042.

A visit to the US Naval Air Station in the western portion of Pensacola at the southern end of Navy Boulevard can also be quite interesting. Open daily from 9 am to 5 pm. Admission is free of charge; Information: Tel: (904) 452-2311. Within this complex, the United States Naval Aviation Museum is especially worth seeing. Among the 50 aircrafts, all of which played a significant role in the development of aeronautics and aerospace, are the NC-4, the first aircraft to cross the Atlantic in 1919; the Skylab Commanders' Capsule; and the F6F Hellcat, the most famous fighter plane from the Second World War. During the main tourist season from June to September, an informative film is presented. One should allow at least two hours for a visit to this museum. Open daily from 9 am to 5 pm; admission is free of charge. Information: Tel: (904) 452-3604.

Pensacola / Practical Information

Accommodation

Camping: Big Lagoon State Recreation Area, 104 tent and RV sites, $10 for four persons, 12301 Gulf Beach Highway; Tel: (904) 492-1595.
Pensacola/Perdido Bay/Lillian KOA, 33951 Spinnaker in Lillian, $15 to $19 for two persons, additional person $1.50; Tel: (205) 962-2727.

Hotels/Motels: Comfort Inn, 6919 Pensacola Boulevard, $35 to $65 for one and two persons (depending on the season), additional person $4; Tel: (904) 478-4499.

Econo Lodge, 7226 Plantation Road, $35 to $45 for one and two persons, additional person $4; Tel: (904) 474-1060.

Executive Inn, 6954 Pensacola Boulevard, $35 to $50 for one and two persons (depending on the season), additional person $4; Tel: (904) 478-4015.

Knights Inn, Northcross Lane, $40 to $60 for one and two persons, additional person $3; Tel: (904) 477-2554.

Red Roof Inn, 7340 Plantation Road $35 to $45 for one and two persons, additional person $4; Tel: (904) 476-7960.

Regal 8 Inn, 7827 North Davis Highway, $35 to $55 for one and two persons; Tel: (904) 476-5386.

Museums: The Pensacola Historical Museum at 405 South Adams Street is housed in one of the oldest churches in Florida. Open Monday to Saturday from 9:30 am to 4:30 pm, free admission; Information: Tel: (904) 433-1559.

The Pensacola Museum of Art, 407 South Jefferson Street, is housed in the former municipal prison. Open Tuesday to Saturday from 10 am to 5 pm, free admission; Information: Tel: (904) 432-6247.

Restaurants: Cap'n Jim's, 905 East Gregory Street, specialising in fish and seafood, inexpensive, closed Sundays; Tel: (904) 433-3562.

Steak & Ale, 920 East Gregory Street, specialising in steaks and seafood, medium price category, reservations are recommended; Tel: (904) 432-1309.

The Oyster Bar, 709 North Boulevard, specialising in seafood, inexpensive, closed Tuesdays; Tel: (904) 455-3925.

Sports and Recreation

Dog Races: Pensacola Greyhound Track, Inc., 951 Dogtrack Road (Highway 98 West), Pensacola, Florida 32506; Tel: (904) 455-8595.

Transportation

Distances from Pensacola to:

Jacksonville — 360 miles
St. Augustine — 388 miles
St. Petersburg — 427 miles
Daytona Beach — 432 miles
Orlando — 438 miles
John F. Kennedy Space Center — 474 miles
Fort Myers — 550 miles

Fort Lauderdale — 638 miles
Miami — 661 miles
Key West — 800 miles

Important Addresses

Police, Fire and Emergency: Tel: 911

Tourist Information:

Pensacola Area Chamber of Commerce, Convention and Visitor Information Center, 1401 East Gregory Street, Pensacola, Florida 32501; Tel: (904) 434-1234.

Seville Quarter, 130 East Government Street, Pensacola, Florida 32501; Tel: (904) 433-7436.

The People of Florida

In addition to the nickname "The Sunshine State," Florida has also been dubbed "God's Waiting Room" or "The Nursing Home of the Nation." The tendency continues for numerous Americans who have left the work force to settle in Florida for their latter years. A demographic study on the age pyramid in the USA reveals that the residents of the cities of Sarasota and Brandonton on the western coast of Florida have the highest average age in the nation. Other cities in Florida trail only slightly. The state of Florida is on average the "oldest state" in the union.

According to the statistics published in February 1990, there are 12,417,606 residents in Florida. In the southern regions, especially in and around Miami, the growing Latin influence is apparent. For the most part, this sector of the population is made up of residents of Cuban descent who chose Florida as their home due to the close proximity to their homeland. The number of Cubans is not far from reaching the one million mark. Most Cubans live in Miami, where the area around 8th Street has been dubbed "Little Havana." The "Anglos" are hardly represented at all in this area.

Photography

Florida is a paradise for photographers — amateur and professional alike. The sunshine state has beautiful landscapes, colourful animals and imaginative theme parks. Film is available everywhere in Florida. One should, however, protect film from the hot climate of Florida. A good place for it is in a refrigerator or on the air conditioning unit in a hotel. This will extend the life of the film. It is also best to have the film developed in the same general area it was purchased since there could be differences in colour.

Police

The police in Florida are very helpful and friendly toward visitors, which is quite a crass contrast to the picture painted of them in films and on television. Municipal police cars are green and white, while the Florida Highway Patrol cars are black and white. Speed limits are strictly enforced and violations can be quite expensive →(Speed Limits).

The police can be reached by phoning the emergency number 911.
→Crime, Theft

Politics

The government of the State of Florida is comprised of the legislative, executive and judicial branches. The capital city and administrative center is in Tallahassee in the northwestern portion of Florida. The State Governor is the highest state government official. The legislative branch is made up of a senate and a house of representatives. Senators are elected every four years and representatives are elected every two years.

Postal System

Generally speaking, post offices are open from Monday to Friday from 8 am to 5 or 6 pm depending on the local business hours; Saturdays, from 8 am to noon. Post offices are closed Sundays and holidays. In some of the large metropolitan areas, post offices offer 24 hour service.

For those sending overseas letters, these usually take 5 to 10 days to reach their destinations. Overseas letters cost 45 cents, post cards, 36 cents; within the United States, postcards cost 15 cents and letters cost 25 cents. Postage stamps are available at post offices, in many hotels, airports and even some supermarkets. In addition, there are some postage stamp vending machines, but these charge around 10% more than the value of the stamps.

Visitors to Florida can have letters and parcels shipped to them by general delivery. General delivery letters and parcels must be claimed within 30 days of receipt. One must present a valid form of identification like a driving licence or passport.

Public Transportation

The public transportation system in Florida is usually a combination of subways, elevated street cars and buses. It is very good and inexpensive. The buses and or trains depart quite often and as a rule cost up to $1 on any given route. Transfers are available from the drivers and are usually free of charge. Exact change is, however, required.

Restaurants

Florida has restaurants to suit just about every taste and budget, from coffee shops, truck stops and fast food restaurants to exclusive restaurants which rank among the best in the world. One will find the ethnic diversity of this state reflected in the selection of restaurants, with ethnic specialties available from around the world, often served in an authentic atmosphere. This is especially true for Little Havana in Miami.

Among the seafood specialities worth recommending, the stone crabs are among the most popular and typical to Florida, and if one has difficulties in deciding then one can never go wrong in ordering the seafood platter.

In most of the restaurants in the middle and upper price categories, it is often recommended or even necessary to make reservations. The prices for restaurants can vary greatly, not only depending on the restaurant itself, but on the location as well. To offer orientation, breakfast ranges from $2 to $8; lunch from $8 to $16. Dinners start at around $10.

St. Augustine

Population: 14,000

Founded in 1565 by the Spaniard Pedro Menendez, St. Augustine is considered the oldest city in the United States. This city, rich in history with a European flair is especially impressive because of San Augustine's Spanish Quarter Antiguo and the massive fortress complex Castillo de San Marcos National Monument from the 16th century at the entrance to the Mantanzas Bay. This fortress, which was never to be conquered, now houses a museum dedicated to the history of the fortress as well as the city. Admission: $1, seniors and visitors under 17 years of age free of charge; Information: Tel: (904) 829-6506. The Spanish Quarter is a reflection of the lifestyle and atmosphere during colonial times not only thanks to its renovated buildings but also especially due to its residents who wear traditional costumes of that period. Admission for all of the buildings: $4 for adults and $1.50 for visitors from 6 to 18 years of age; Tel: (904) 825-6830.

The St. Augustine Sightseeing Train takes visitors on a tour through the old district of the city. Tickets for adults cost $9 and $4 for children from 6 to 12 years of age; 170 San Marco Avenue, Tel: (904) 829-6545.

South of the city on the A1A is one of the oldest alligator farms in Florida. Crocodiles, alligators and other wild animals are kept and bred here as well. One should allow around two hours for a visit to this alligator farm. Open daily from 9 am to 5:30 pm. Shows are presented hourly. Admission: $7.95 for adults and $5.95 for children from 3 to 11 years of age; Tel: (904) 824-3337.

Eighteen miles further south on the A1A is Marineland of Florida, with various shows with trained dolphins and porpoises as well as seals. One should allow four hours for a visit to Marineland. Open daily from 9 am to 4 pm and 9 am to 6 pm from September to May. Admission: $12 for adults and $7 for children from 3 to 11 years of age. Information: Marineland of Florida, 9507 Ocean Shore Boulevard, Marineland, Florida 32086-9602; Tel: (904) 471-1111.

State Parks: Anastasia State Recreational Area, 5 Anastasia Park Drive, St. Augustine, Florida 32085; Tel: (904) 471-3033.

Faver-Dykes State Park, Route 4, Box 213-J-1, St. Augustine, Florida 32086; Tel: (904) 794-0997.

The fort Castillo de San Marcos (16th Century) now houses a museum

Washington Oaks State Gardens, Route 1, P.O. Box 128-A, St. Augustine, Florida 32086; Tel: (904) 445-3161.

St. Augustine / Practical Information

Accommodation

Camping: Anastasia State Recreation Area, 139 tent and RV sites, $10 per site, 5 Anastasia Park Drive; Tel: (904) 471-3033.

St. Augustine KOA, 112 tent and RV sites, swimming pool, $18 to $23 for one and two persons, additional person $4, reservations are recommended, 9950 KOA Road; Tel: (904) 824-8309.

St. Augustine Beach KOA, 136 tent and RV sites, swimming pool, $16 to $19 for one and two persons, additional person $2, reservations are recommended, 525 West Pope Road; Tel: (904) 471-3113 and 1-800-992-5622.

St. Augustine Ocean Road Resort, 140 tent and RV sites, large swimming pool, $20 to $28 for five persons, additional person $2, 4850 A1A South, reservations are recommended; Tel: (904) 471-3353.

Four Seasons RV Park, 58 tent and RV sites, from $20, 2770 State Road 16, reservations are recommended; Tel: (904) 829-3108.

Stagecoach RV Park, 46 RV sites, from $18, 2711 County Road 208, reservations are recommended; Tel: (904) 824-2319.

Cooksey's Camping Resort, 199 tent and RV sites, swimming pool, from $18, 2795 State Road 3 in St. Augustine Beach, reservations are recommended; Tel: (904) 471-3171.

Hotels/Motels: Ponce de Leon Resort, 4000 US Highway 1 North, $60 to $145 for one and two persons, additional person $6, reservations are recommended; Tel: (904) 824-2821.

San Marco Inn, 231 San Marco Avenue, $45 to $85 for one and two persons, additional person $5; Tel: (904) 829-3321.

Scottish Inn, I-95 and State Road 16, $30 to $50 for one and two persons, additional person $5; Tel: (904) 829-5643.

Sunshine Inn, I95 and State Road 16, $30 to $50 for one and two persons, additional person $5; Tel: (904) 824-4436.

Restaurants: The Chimes Restaurant, Avenida Menendez; Tel: (904) 829-8141.

Columbia Restaurant, 98 St. George Street, offering entertainment some evenings, reservations are recommended; Tel: (904) 824-1905.

Raintree Restaurant, 102 San Marcos Avenue, excellent fish and seafood, reservations are recommended; Tel: (904) 824-7211.

Transportation

Distances from St. Augustine to:

Jacksonville — 25 miles
Daytona Beach — 33 miles
Orlando — 61 miles
John F. Kennedy Space Center — 116 miles
St. Petersburg — 125 miles
Fort Myers — 157 miles
Fort Lauderdale — 177 miles
Miami — 193 miles
Pensacola — 242 miles
Key West — 511 miles

Important Addresses

St. Augustine Chamber of Commerce, P.O. Box, Drawer O, St. Augustine, Florida 32085; Tel: (904) 829-5681.

St. Petersburg

Population: 240,000

The city of St. Petersburg in Russia was the inspiration for this city's name when Peter Demens named this city after his birthplace. This took place in 1885, over 40 years after the first settlement was founded at this location. The railway, built by Peter Demens was also instrumental in the development of this city.

Today, St. Petersburg counts among the tourist centers of Florida. Owing to of its sunny climate, it has been given the epithet "Sunshine City." This is complemented by the city's beautiful location on the southern tip of the Pinellas Peninsula, framed by Tampa Bay to the east and the Gulf of Mexico to the west.

St. Petersburg / Sights

Fort De Soto Park: The six islands of Madeline, St. Jean, St. Christopher, Bonne Fortune, Scratch and Mullet comprise this park measuring almost 10,000 acres in total area. The plants and animals within this park fall under legal protection. On the southernmost point on Mullet Key is a fort from the Spanish-American War; Tel: (813) 462-3347.

Pier Place, 800 Second Avenue Northeast. This square is famous for its five story inverted pyramid. This architecturally bold shopping center is located in a part of the city with a very pleasant atmosphere. This area includes an auditorium, a sports stadium, boat docks, a beach promenade and of course numerous shops, restaurants and boutiques. This area of the city has its own special flair; Tel: (813) 893-7437.

Salvador Dali Museum, 100 Third Street South. This museum houses the world's most extensive collection of works by the famous Spanish artist. The collection includes 93 oil paintings, 200 watercolours and sketches and over 1,000 graphics, sculptures and other objects. Open from Tuesday to Saturday 10 am to 5 pm, Sundays noon to 5 pm, closed Mondays. Admission: $4 for adults and $2.50 for students. Information: Salvador Dali Museum, 1000 Third Street South, St. Petersburg, Florida 33701; Tel: (813) 823-3767.

Sunken Gardens: 1825 Fourth Street North. This park with thousands of exotic plants and plants indigenous to the region is the result of one man's initiative about 70 years ago. He dug the basin for a lake and then used the fertile soil to lay out the gardens. Today, the sunken gardens are among the most significant attractions in St. Petersburg. One should allow two hours for a visit to the sunken gardens. Open daily from 9 am to 5:30 pm. Admission: $6.95 for adults and $4 for children from 3 to 11 years of age; Tel: (813) 896-3186.

Tiki Gardens, 19601 Gulf Boulevard north of Indian Shores. This Polynesian park offers a divers picture of the culture and religion of Polynesia. Those who are interested in foreign religions should definitely plan a visit to Tiki gardens, allowing four hours. Open daily from 10 am to 6 pm. Admission: $3 for adults, $1.50 for children from 3 to 11 years of age; Tel: (813) 595-2567.

St. Petersburg / Practical Information

Accommodation

Camping: Fort De Soto Park Campground, 235 tent and RV sites, $10 for two persons, located at the southern end of the Pinella Bayway; Tel: (813) 866-2662.

St. Petersburg KOA, 475 tent and RV sites, swimming pool, $20 to $30 for two persons (depending on the season), additional person $5, 5400 95th street North, reservations are recommended; Tel: (813) 392-2233.

Clearwater-Tarpon Springs KOA, 115 tent and RV sites, heated swimming pool, $22 for one and two persons, additional person $4, 3906 US 19 North in Palm Harbor; Tel: (813) 937-8412.

Hotels/Motels: Bayway Motor Lodge, 3501 54th Avenue South, $45 to $65 for one and two persons (depending on the season), additional person $6; Tel: (813) 867-3171.

Empress Motel Apartments, 1503 9th Street North, $45 to $65 for one and two persons (depending on the season), additional person $5, apartments for four persons $50 to $70 (depending on the season), reservations are recommended; Tel: (813) 894-0635.

Grant Hotel & Apartments, 9046 4th Street North, $40 to $65 for one and two persons (depending on the season), additional person $6, apartments for four persons $170 to $200 or $245 to $295 per week (depending on the season), reservations are recommended; Tel: (813) 576-1369.

Kentucky Derby Motel, 4246 4th Street North, from $35 for one and two persons, additional person $6, reservations are recommended; Tel: (813) 526-7373.

La Mark Charles Motel, 6200 34th Street North, $40 to $60 for one and two persons (depending on the season), additional person $6, reservations are recommended; Tel: (813) 527-7334.

Pennsylvania Hotel 300 4th Street North, $40 to $60 for one and two persons (depending on the season), additional person $6, reservations are recommended; Tel: (813) 822-4045.

A touch of the exclusive can be found along the Sun Coast

St. Petersburg

Beaches: The bathing area for this city is on the Gulf Coast west of St. Petersburg, from Fort De Soto Park all the way to Clearwater Beach. The most popular area are the beaches St. Petersburg Beach/Treasure Island, Madeira Beach, North Redington Beach and Indian Rocks Beach.

Night Life and Entertainment: St. Petersburg has a large number of bars and pubs which offer entertainment. Most of these can be found in the hotels along the beach. More detailed information can be found in the magazine "Guide" which is available at most every hotel reception desk free of charge. In addition, information on entertainment and special events can be found in the entertainment sections of the two local daily newspapers, the "St. Petersburg Evening Independent" and the "Clearwater Sun."

Restaurants

Bradford's Coach House Restaurant, 1900 4th Street North, popular restaurant with reasonable prices, closed Mondays; Tel: (813) 822-7982.

Crabby Bill's, 409 Gulf Boulevard, at Indian Rocks Beach, excellent fish and seafood, reasonable prices; Tel: (813) 595-4825.

Pepin, 4125 4th Street, restaurant specialising in Spanish cuisine; Tel: (813) 821-3773.

Silas Dent's, 5501 Gulf Boulevard in St. Petersburg Beach, an excellent restaurant for fish and seafood, offers live entertainment on occasion, reservations are recommended; Tel: (813) 360-6961.

Sightseeing

Bus Tours: First Class Coach Co./American Sightseeing, 2922 46th Avenue North, St. Petersburg, Florida 33714; Tel: (813) 526-9086.

Gulf Coast Gray Line, P.O. Box 145, 921 Third Street South, St. Petersburg, Florida 33731; Tel: (813) 822-3577.

The Limo, Inc., 11901 30th Court North, St. Petersburg, Florida 33716; Tel: (813) 572-1111.

Sun Lines, 870 74th Avenue North, St. Petersburg, Florida 33702; Tel: (813) 525-7199.

Sightseeing Tours by Boat: the tour boats depart from Municipal Marina on Vinoy Basin. Grayline Water Tours operate twice daily at 11:30 am and 2 pm, departing on two-hour tours. Information: Pier 401 2nd Avenue Northeast; Tel: (813) 823-8171 or (813) 823-1665. The tours aboard the "Belle of St. Petersburg" offer diversity and cost between $6 and $18.

The "Captain Anderson" departs from the Gulf Coast, Dolphin Village Shopping Center, St. Petersburg Beach; Tel: (813) 360-2619, and the "Captain Anderson II," Clearwater Beach Marina; Tel: (813) 462-2628.

Sports and Recreation

Boating: Rental boats are available in almost every size at the rental agencies along Tampa Bay or the Gulf. Addresses can be found in the yellow pages of the local telephone book.

Dog Races: From the beginning of January to the beginning of May, dog races take place in the Derby Lane Dogtrack. The entrance to the Dog Track is located at 10490 Gandy Boulevard. Tel: (813) 576-1361.

Fishing: Those who enjoy fishing will find a paradise awaiting them in Florida. From freshwater to deep-sea fishing — this state has everything to offer. One does, however, need the appropriate fishing licence. Licences along with the informative brochure "Guide to Florida Fishing" are available in sporting goods stores. During January and February, the St. Petersburg Rod and Gun Club offer fishing courses on Maggiore Lake free of charge. This is also a good place to acquire more detailed information on fishing.

Golf: Public golf courses can be found on Mangrove Bay, 62nd Avenue, north of Ulmerton Road, near St. Petersburg-Clearwater Airport, on 22nd Avenue South west of Kingston. Further addresses can be found in the yellow pages of the local telephone book.

Swimming: →Beaches, this entry

Tennis: Public tennis courts can be found in Bartlett, Crisp, Azalea and Gladden Parks.

Transportation

Trains: Amtrak Station, 3601 31st Street North; Tel: (813) 522-9475.

Buses: The public bus routes operated by the Pinellas Suncoast Transit Authority not only serve the city of St. Petersburg, but the entire County of Pinellas. Information: Tel: (813) 530-9911.

Greyhound Terminal: 110 Central Avenue; Tel: (813) 895-4455.

Continental Trailways Terminal: 105 2nd Street South; Tel: (813) 823-3140.

Distances from St. Petersburg to:

Orlando — 66 miles

Fort Myers — 69 miles

John F. Kennedy Space Center — 142 miles

Daytona Beach — 160 miles

St. Augustine — 198 miles

Jacksonville — 209 miles

Fort Lauderdale — 235 miles

Miami — 246 miles

Key West — 380 miles

Pensacola — 437 miles

Airport: The Tampa International Airport (TPA) is located eight miles west of Tampa. Limousine service operates between the airport and downtown St. Petersburg. This service costs $8 to $9.

Airport Information: Tel: (813) 276-3400.

The St. Petersburg/Clearwater International Airport (PIE) is located 7 miles southeast of Clearwater directly on Old Tampa Bay. Information: Tel: (813) 531-1451.

Taxi: Fares in St. Petersburg range around $1.70 for the first mile and $1 for each additional mile.

Important Addresses

Good informational materials are available by contacting:

Pinellas County Tourist Development Council, Newport Square, 4625 East Bay Drive, Suite 109A, Clearwater, Florida 34624; Tel: (813) 530-6452.

The St. Petersburg Chamber of Commerce operates tourist information offices at 401 3rd Avenue South; Tel: (813) 821-4069, and directly on the Pier, 800 2nd Avenue Northeast; Tel: (813) 821-4715.

There is also a Suncoast Welcome Center at 2001 Ulmerton Road; Tel: (813) 576-1449.

Sales Tax

Florida's state tax is presently 6%. Individual counties can levy an additional 1% and an additional percentage may be levied on food, entertainment and accommodation in some areas as a tourist development tax.

Sarasota

Population: 50,000

The city of Sarasota at the center of the west coast, sees itself as the cultural capital of the state of Florida. This reputation is based predominantly on the past benevolence of the legendary John and Mable Ringling. In 1927, they chose Sarasota as their residence and immediately began construction on a Venetian palace for themselves as well as their extensive collection of art. The house was left to the state and is now a part of the Ringling Museum of Art Complex.

Sarasota / Sights

Ringling Museum of Art Complex: This museum is comprised of the Museum of Circus, The Ringling Residence Ca'd'Zan, which, translated from the Venetian, means "House of John," and the Asolo Theater. Asolo is a town near

Venice in which this theater was built at the end of the 18th century. It was then dismantled during the 1930's and reconstructed on this site in the 1950's. By dialling the telephone number (813) 355-5137, one can get information on the current program offered in the Ringling Complex. The Art Museum has the largest collection of works by Rubens in the world, while the Circus Museum keeps the golden age of circus alive. In total, one should allow three to four hours for a visit to the Ringling Complex. Open Friday to Wednesday from 10 am to 6 pm, Thursdays from 10 am to 11 pm. Admission: $8.50 for adults, children under 13 free of charge, with free admission to the Art Museum on Saturdays.

Information: The Ringling Museum of Art, 5401 Bay Shore Road, Sarasota, Florida 33578; Tel: (813) 355-5101.

Belim's Cars & Music of Yesterday, 5500 North Tamiami Trail. This museum, with around 170 classic and antique automobiles as well as the world's most extensive collection of mechanical musical instruments is definitely worth a visit. One should allow about two hours. Open daily from 8:30 am to 6 pm. Admission: $6.50 for adults and $3.25 for children from 6 to 12 years of age. Tel: (813) 355-6228.

Sarasota Jungle Gardens, 3701 Bayshore Road, south of the Sarasota Bradenton Airport. This nature park with its tropical plants and numerous animals in not only popular with nature lovers but photographers as well. Performances with reptiles and birds take place four times daily. Open daily from 9 am to 5 pm; admission: $7 for adults and $3.50 for children from 3 to 12 years of age. Information: Tel: (813) 355-5305.

Myakka River State Park: nature lovers should definitely visit the Myakka River State Park, 9 miles east of the city at 132007 State Road 72. One can enjoy this park by car, by tram by boat and even by renting a bicycle. Information: Tel: (813) 924-1027.

Sarasota / Practical Information

Accommodation

Camping: Camper Land Sun-N-Fun Resort, 1707 RV sites, larger heated pool, from $18 for two persons, additional person $2, 7125 Fruitville Road, reservations are recommended; Tel: (813) 371-2505.

Gulf Beach Travel Trailer Park, 50 tent and RV sites, $18 to $26 for three persons, additional person $2 to $3 (depending on the season), 8862 Midnight Pass Road, reservations are recommended; Tel: (813) 349-3839.

Myakka River State Park, 76 tent and RV sites, $8 for four persons (→Sights, this entry); Tel: (813) 924-1027.

Pine Shores Trailer Park, 42 RV sites, from $22 for two persons, additional person $3, reservations are recommended, 6450 South Tamiami Trail; Tel: (813) 922-1929.

Hotels/Motels: Bel Air Motel, 1080 North Tamiami Trail, $40 to $65 for one and two persons, additional person $5 to $8 (depending on the season), reservations are recommended; Tel: (813) 953-7544.

Cadillac Motel, 4201 North Tamiami Trail, $40 to $70 for one and two persons (depending on the season), additional person $4; Tel: (813) 355-7108.

Sarasota Motor Inn, 8150 North Tamiami Trail, $45 to $60 for one and two persons (depending on the season), additional person $4; Tel: (813) 355-7747.

Airport: The Sarasota-Bradenton Airport (SRQ) is located around 3 miles north of the city.

Information: Tel: (813) 355-2761.

Restaurants: Zinn's Restaurant, 6101 North Tamiami Trail, interesting atmosphere, good food, reservations are recommended; Tel: (813) 355-5417.

Important Addresses

Greater Sarasota Tourism Association, 655 North Tamiami Trail, Sarasota, Florida 34236; Tel: (813) 957-1877.

Shopping

The shopping in Florida is diverse but can also be quite expensive, depending on where one shops. Just about everything imaginable is available. Of course, the typical souvenirs can be found at the individual attractions or larger cities.

In the larger tourist centers there are numerous shopping centers, some of which are attractions in and of themselves.

Most supermarkets are open 24 hours, seven days a week.

Sights

The state of Florida is incredibly diverse and attractive in terms of what it has to offer tourists. In order to provide a better orientation, the regions of Florida are described in more detail below.

The Northwest

The panhandle in the northwest of Florida reflects the old traditions of the south which can still be seen and experienced in many places. From the historical city of Pensacola in the west to the lively fishing town of Cedar City, there is a strip of beach that seems to be endless. This beach is quite heavily frequented all the way to Panama City and it is being increasingly developed for tourism. Secluded beaches can be found further to the east and to the south. At the Great Bend, however, the beaches disappear, being replaced by grassy Gulf savanna landscape. Located in these regions are fishing towns with fantastic seafood restaurants and secluded palm islands. Not far to the north of Cedar Key, the beautiful and churning Suwanee River with its characteristic brown water empties into the Gulf of Mexico. This river is among the few untouched rivers in the United States, having never been used commercially. The rolling hills in the interior of the northwestern regions of Florida is characterised by large expanses and huge pine forests, which offer the paper processing industry a seemingly endless reserve. Amid this landscape of hills is the city of Tallahassee, Florida's capital.

Travel Destinations: Cedar Key, Panama City, Pensacola, Tallahassee, Wakulla Springs.

The Northeast
Northeastern Florida is rich in history, taking visitors back to the times of the former Spanish and British colonies in some places. This period in history is especially well preserved in St. Augustine, which calls itself the oldest city in the United States. Tourism also began to lay roots in the northeastern regions of Florida. Today, tourists are attracted by the historical significance of this region and the magnificent beaches, famous for its dunes, its beautiful surf and its solid sand. The northern extremes of Florida is also the point of origin of the legendary Road A1A leading to Miami.

Travel Destinations: Jacksonville, St. Augustine.

The Central Western Coast
Tampa Bay cuts into this region, which, for a long time, was a very secluded area in Florida. The Bay is now the main tourist attraction in this region. The big cities of Tampa and St. Petersburg offer activity and diversity, whereby Pinellas County west of Tampa Bay hosts the most visitors annually. This area with hotels and marketed beaches is hardly distinguishable any more from the Gold Coast in the south. The coastline continues to be developed to the south. Those in search of a secluded beach will have to look further to the north in the central regions of the western coast and a good portion of luck

is also necessary. The fantastic beaches, the favorable climate and the lush vegetation make for the attractions of this region in terms of tourism.
Travel Destinations: Tampa, St. Petersburg, Sarasota, Tarpon Springs.

Central Florida
From Ocala National Forest to the huge Lake Okeechobee is the heartland of Florida — meanwhile also a focal point of tourism. However neither the landscapes nor the lakes are the main attractions in this region of Florida. This has long since been surpassed by the home of Mickey Mouse, the World of Walt Disney, which has boosted Orlando to the largest tourist center on earth. In 1987 alone, almost 25 million visitors came to this city. It is, therefore, not surprising that other attractions can also exist quite well in this area. Among these are Sea World, Circus World, Universal Studios, Cypress Gardens, Silver Springs near Ocala and of course the inevitable alligator farms of Florida.
Travel Destinations: Orlando, Silver Springs, Winter Haven

The lush vegetation is one of the main attractions of Florida

The Central Eastern Coast

The central eastern coast of Florida has long since become a transit route for those travelling on the A1A. Others take a trip from Orlando to the John F. Kennedy Space Center or to the famous automobile races at Daytona Beach. These two points remain the main attractions of this reason today; however, the growing number of hotel complexes, especially to the south of the space center are evidence that this section of coastline has a lot to offer holiday travellers.

Travel Destinations: Daytona Beach, John F. Kennedy Space Center.

The Southwest

From Port Charlotte in the north to Flamingo in the southern Everglades, the southwestern region of Florida offers a vary diverse coastline. Beaches, which are seeing an ever increasing number of hotels being built, shell banks on Captiva and Sanibel Islands, pristine mangrove islands and the incomparable Everglades — home to the countless species of birds, the alligators and crocodiles — all can be found in Florida's southwest.

Travel Destinations: Fort Myers, Captiva Island, Sanibel, Everglades City.

The Southeast

The southeastern coastline of Florida, beginning at Palm Beach in the north and ending with the chain of 42 Florida Keys including Key West, is famous worldwide as a holiday destination. The rush to this southeastern extremity of the United States was so huge that the Gold Coast from Palm Beach, including Fort Lauderdale and Hollywood to Miami and Miami Beach would experience a dramatic urbanisation, the like of which remains unknown to any other region of the United States. The climate, the beaches and that which the cities have to offer make for the attraction of this region. Not to be forgotten is the Cuban atmosphere and charm of the Florida Keys — especially Key West — and Everglades National Park. These factors make this region a preferred destination, not only within the state of Florida, but for all of the United States.

Travel Destinations: Biscayne National Park, Everglades National Park, Key West, Miami/Miami Beach, Fort Lauderdale, Florida Keys, Key Largo, Homestead, Palm Beach/West Palm Beach.

Silver Springs

The natural spring region of Silver Springs is approximately 6¼ miles east of Ocala on the State Road 40. It was compared with a utopia even by the earliest settlers. Even today, many visitors consider this wilderness with crystal clear lakes and an extraordinary wealth of wildlife for one of the last paradises on earth. A trip through the jungle with a glass bottom boat on the Silver River and Crystal Lake is among the special attractions that Silver Springs has to offer. One should plan on more than a brief visit to this area, allowing four to five hours time. Open daily from 9 am to 5:30 pm with extended hours during the summer season and weekends. Admission: $19.95 for adults and $14.95 for children from 3 to 10 years of age. Information: Tel: (904) 236-2121.

Silver Springs / Practical Information
Accommodation
Camping: Ben's Hitching Post Campground, 35 tent and RV sites, from $14 for four persons, additional person $2, located on State Road 40 approximately 6 miles east of the springs, reservations are recommended; Tel: (904) 625-4213. Silver Springs Campers Garden, 184 tent and RV sites, from $18 for four persons, additional person $2, on State Road 40 directly opposite the springs, reservations are recommended; Tel: (904) 236-3700.

Hotels/Motels: Spring Side Motel, 5350 East Silver Spring Boulevard, $30 to $45 for one and two persons (depending on the season), additional person $3, reservations are recommended; Tel: (904) 236-2788.
Stage Stop Inn, 5131 East Silver Spring Boulevard, $35 to $50 for one and two persons (depending on the season), additional person $4, reservations are recommended; Tel: (904) 236-2501.

Speed Limits

Outside of city limits, the speed limit is 55 miles per hour (88 kilometres per hour). When driving through less populated areas, 65 mph is allowed (104 kmph). Within city limits, speed limits are from 25 to 30 mph (40 to 48 kmph) or as posted. One should definitely adhere to these regulations because speeding violations can be quite costly.

Sports and Recreation

In Florida, as well as the rest of the United States, sports and recreational activities play a very important role. Football, baseball and basketball are the most popular spectator sports and mobilise masses. In addition, specifically in Florida, Jai Alai, dog, horse and automobile races are extremely popular. Recreational sports play a very important role in Florida, the holiday capital of the US.

Information on sporting events and public sports facilities is available at visitor information bureaus or in the sports section of the local newspapers.

The popularity of sports in Florida is reflected by the diversity of the types of sports and recreation offered. Due to the natural conditions present in Florida, those types of sports are emphasised that have to do with water. These include swimming, surfing, scuba diving, water skiing, fishing and of course boating.

Ideal conditions for swimming can be found all along the seemingly endless coastline of Florida, but also at the inland lakes. Most surfers prefer the much higher waves on the Atlantic Coast of Florida over the milder surf on the Gulf of Mexico. Scuba divers and snorkellers will find a veritable paradise at the Florida Keys. Water skiers will find the best conditions near the tourist centers. Fishing is also a very popular type of recreational sport in Florida. One will see people fishing almost everywhere, on the beaches or at one of the multitude of inland lakes. The proper equipment for a fishing expedition can be rented at a number of places. Types of fishing possible in Florida range from deep-sea fishing to fresh and saltwater fishing — the possibilities are limitless.

Motor boats, sail boats and canoes can also be rented in a number of places. There are also a number of fantastic routes in Florida — in the Florida Keys or the Everglades, to name only two. Of course, the Jetski has long since become a common sight along the coast as well.

Golf is yet another of the most popular sports in Florida. In Florida alone, there are over 750 golf courses and there are even more tennis courts — tennis lessons (also for beginners) are offered in the tourist centers.

Horse and greyhound races are enjoying an ever increasing popularity. Of course, wagers are also accepted on these races. The Mecca for automobile racing has been Daytona Beach for many years, where the races took place on the solid sand of the beach before the Daytona International Speedway was built.

Jai Alai is quite a spectacular type of sport, also famous as the fastest sport using a ball in the world. One can either take a seat as a spectator or join the game as a "Pelotari" (a participant).

Those who would like further information on the various types of sports and recreation offered in Florida can contact the following addresses:

Boating: Florida Boaters Association, 1900 79th Street Causeway, North Bay Village, Florida 33141; Tel: (305) 868-4117.

Florida Sailing Association, Inc., 1941 Arrowhead Drive Northeast, St. Petersburg, Florida 33703; Tel: (813) 526-0810.

Dog Racing: Pompano Beach, 1800 Southwest 3rd Street.

Casselberry (near Orlando), Seminole Greyhound Park, 200 Seminola Boulevard.

Longwood (near Orlando), Sanford-Orlando Kennel Club, Dog Track Road.

Daytona Beach, Daytona Beach Kennel Club, 2201 Volusia Avenue.

Jacksonville, Jacksonville Kennel Club, 1440 North McDuff Avenue.

Key West, Keys Racing Association, Stock Island.

Miami, Biscayne Dog Track, 320 Northwest 115th Street.

Pensacola Greyhound Park, Dog Track Road.

St Petersburg, Derby Land, 10490 Candy Boulevard North.

Sarasota Kennel Club, 5400 Bradenton Road.

Tampa, Tampa Greyhound Track, 8300 North Nebraska Avenue.

West Palm Beach Kennel Club, 1111 North Congress Avenue.

Fishing is a popular pastime in Florida — whether at high seas or simply on a quiet section of coastline

Fishing: Game and Fresh Water Fish Commission, Ferris Bryant Building, Tallahassee, Florida 32301; Tel: (904) 488-1960.

In Northwestern Florida: Tel: (904) 265-3676.

In Northeastern Florida: Tel: (904) 752-0353.

In Central Florida: Tel: (904) 629-8162.

In Southern Florida: Tel: (813) 686-8157.

In the Everglades: Tel: (305) 683-0748.

Football: Miami Dolphins, 477 Biscayne Boulevard, Miami, Florida 33137; Tel: (305) 576-1000.

Tampa Bay Buccaneers, 1 Buccaneer Place, Tampa, Florida 33607; Tel: (813) 872-7977.

Golf: Florida State Golf Association (PGA), 106 Avenue of the Champions, Palm Beach Gardens, Florida 33410; Tel: (305) 626-3600.

Amateur Golf Association, 5555 Hollywood Boulevard, Hollywood, Florida 33021; Tel: (305) 983-6554.

A surfer's paradise: in Florida, surfers will definitely get their money's worth

Horse Racing: Hialeah Park (near Miami), 105 East 21st Street.
Miami, Calder Race Course, 21001 Northwest 27th Avenue.
Oldsmar (near Tampa), Tampa Bay Downs, Racetrack Road.
Jai Alai: Dania (near Fort Lauderdale), Dania Jai-Alai Palace, 301 Dania Beach Boulevard.
Daytona Beach, Volusia Jai-Alai Fronton US Highway 92.
Fern Park (near Orlando).
Florida Jai-Alai, 211 US Highway 17-92.
Miami, Miami Jai-Alai, 3500 Northwest 37th Avenue.
Tampa, Tampa Jai-Alai, 5125 South Dale Mabry Highway.
West Palm Beach, Palm Beach Jai-Alai Fronton, 1415 45th Street.
Polo: Palm Beach Polo and Country Club, 13198 Forest Hill Boulevard, West Palm Beach, Florida 33414; Tel: (305) 793-1113.
Tennis: U.S. Professional Tennis Association (USPTA), P.O. Box 7046, Wesley Chapel, Florida 34249; Tel: (813) 973-3777.
Florida Tennis Association, 9620 Northeast 2nd Avenue, Miami Shores, Florida 33138; Tel: (305) 757-8568.

Tallahassee

Population: 82,000

Tallahassee has been the capital of Florida since 1823. The State Capitol with its classicist façade originates from this period. The modern, 300 foot high new building makes for an interesting architectural contrast, which seems to be characteristic for this city. There are always reminders of times gone by, whether they be the historical buildings, remnants from the old south like the houses built by the slaves before 1865 or the landscape around Tallahassee. After a ten-hour drive covering around 500 miles from Miami, one will find oneself amid a wooded landscape of gently rolling hills, making up the characteristic profile of this region. In addition, Tallahassee is renowned for its beautiful parks and the lakes in the surrounding regions.

One can gain a better impression of this by visiting the Tallahassee Junior Museum at Bradford Lake with its nature trails through the forests and cypress swamps, a farm from 1880, a reptile house, a nature reserve for Florida's panthers and much more. Admission: $4 for adults; visitors between the ages of 5 and 15 as well as students pay $1.50. Information: Tel: (904) 576-1636.

In the northeastern portion of the city, at 3540 Thomasville Road is the Alfred B. MacLay State Garden. It was founded in 1923 by the New York businessman and includes azaleas, magnolias, camellia and a number of other plants. Admission: from the beginning of January to the end of April, $2 for adults and $1 for children from 6 to 12 years of age and students. During the rest of the year, 50 cents. Information: Tel: (904) 893-4232.

Also worth visiting is the Museum of Florida History at 500 South Bronough Street. Articles exhibited here include historically and archaeologically significant specimens, ranging from gold pieces from the Spanish Conquistadors to a huge mastodon skeleton. Open Monday to Friday from 9 am to 4:30 pm, Saturdays from 10 am to 4:30 pm and Sundays from noon to 4:30 pm; admission is free of charge. Information: Tel: (904) 488-1484.

State Parks: Lake Jackson Mounds State Archeological Site, 1313 Crowder Road, Tallahassee, Florida 32308; Tel: (904) 562-0042.

Lake Talquin State Recreation Area, Star Route 1, P.O. Box 2222, Tallahassee, Florida 32304; Tel: (904) 576-8233.

Tallahassee / Practical Information

Accommodation

Camping: Silver Lake, 25 tent and RV sites, $8 for three persons, located on County Road 260 southwest of the city; Tel: (904) 926-3561.

A Camper's World Campground, 32 tent and RV sites, $16 to $18 for two persons, additional person $3, Route 1 in Lamont, reservations are recommended; Tel: (904) 997-3300.

Tallahassee RV Camping, 73 RV sites, $18 to $20 for two persons, additional person $3, 6504 Mahan Drive, reservations are recommended; Tel: (904) 878-7641.

Hotels/Motels: American Inn, 2726 North Monroe Street, $35 to $45 for one and two persons, additional person $3; Tel: (904) 386-5000.

Best Inns of America, 2738, Graves Road, $40 to $50 for one and two persons; Tel: (904) 562-2378.

Days Inn South, 3100 Apalachee Parkway, $35 to $45 for one and two persons; Tel: (904) 877-6121.

Dutch Inn Motel, 2799 Apalachee Parkway, $30 to $45 for one and two persons, additional person $3; Tel: (904) 877-7813.

Ponce de Leon Motel, 1801 West Tennessee Street, $30 to $40 for one and two persons, additional person $3; Tel: (904) 222-4950.

Restaurants: Tucker's Drive Inn Restaurant, 3520 Woodville Highway, inexpensive.

Silver Slipper, 531 Scotty's Lane, medium price category, reservations are recommended; Tel: (904) 386-9366.

Transportation

Distances from Tallahassee to:

Jacksonville — 164 miles
St. Augustine — 195 miles
Pensacola — 198 miles
Daytona Beach — 235 miles
Orlando — 242 miles
St. Petersburg — 251 miles
John F. Kennedy Space Center — 288 miles
Fort Myers — 356 miles
Fort Lauderdale — 445 miles
Miami — 467 miles
Key West — 607 miles

Airport: Tallahassee Regional Airport (TLH), 3240 Capital Circle Southwest, Tallahassee, Florida 32304; Tel: (904) 5750666. The airport is located about 5 miles southwest of the city.

Important Addresses

Tallahassee Area Convention and Visitors Bureau, P.O. Box 1639, Tallahassee, Florida 32302; Tel: (904) 681-9200 and (904) 224-8116. There is a visitors bureau in the city, located at 100 North Duval Street. It is open Monday to Friday from 8:30 am to 5 pm; Tel: (904) 224-8116.

Leon County Tourist Development Council, Room 108, Leon County Courthouse, Tallahassee, Florida 32301; Tel: (904) 488-3990.

Tampa

Population: 300,000

The origins of Tampa — which is now the third largest city in Florida — go back to Fort Brooke, which was built in 1824 on Tampa Bay during the war with the Seminole Indians. The harbor played a strategically significant role in wars to follow. When Tampa was incorporated into the railway network built by the industrialist Henry B. Plant (the counterpart to Henry M. Flagler's undertakings on the eastern coast), the city grew rapidly. Today, Tampa's harbour is the seventh largest in the United States with a tonnage throughput of 50 million per year. In addition, the cigar factory also plays a significant role in the local economy. Founded in 1886 by Cuban immigrants, this factory produces three million cigars annually.

Tampa / Sights

Busch Gardens, The Dark Continent, 3000 Busch Boulevard between 30th and 40th Street. Africa at the turn of the century is the theme of this amusement park with elephants, zebras, giraffes antelopes and many other animals all able to roam freely within portions of the park. There are also the "Python" and "Scorpion" roller coasters, offering the chance to test one's nerves. One can take a trip over the artificial rapids or enjoy one of the various shows or other attractions. One should allow an entire day for a visit to Busch Gardens. Open daily from 9:30 am to 6 pm with extended hours during the summer months. Admission: $26.45; parking $3. Information: Busch Gardens, P.O. Box 9158, Tampa, Florida 33674; Tel: (813) 977-6606 or (813) 971-8282.

Directly next to Busch Gardens is the *Adventure Island* aquatic park, 4500 Bougainvillea Avenue. Open March 31 to May 25 daily from 10 am to 5 pm, May 26 to August 19 daily from 9 am to 8 pm and August 20 to October 28 from 10 am to 5 pm. Admission: $15.85; Tel: (813) 977-6606.

Ybor City, the Latin Quarter of Tampa, is located between Nebraska Avenue, 22nd Street, Columbus Drive and East Broadway. The name of this district originates from Vicente Martinez Ybor, who brought the first Cuban cigar factory to Tampa at the end of the 19th century. His old cigar factory built of red bricks and pine, cedar and oak has long since been taken over by shops, businesses and theaters. It is now considered a tourist attraction, whereby the original character of the building has remained intact. Today, the factory stands on Ybor Square, the nostalgic center of Ybor City.

Ybor Square, 1901 North 13th Street; Tel: (813) 247-4497.

At 1818 19th Avenue is the *Ybor City State Museum,* housed in a former bakery. There one can gain more information on the history of the local cigar industry. Admission is free of charge; Tel: (813) 247-6323.

Lowry Park Zoo, 7530 North Boulevard. This new zoo is Tampa's newest attraction. Tel: (813) 935-8552.

Henry B. Plant Museum, 401 West Kennedy Boulevard. This building belongs to the University of Tampa and is definitely worth a visit, because of its 13 minarets alone. Admission: $2; Tel: (813) 253-3333.

Museum of Science and Industry, 4801 East Fowler Avenue. Interesting exhibits make fundamental advances in science and technology more understandable. Open daily from 10 am to 4:30 pm. Admission: $4 for adults and $2 for visitors from 5 to 15 years of age; Tel: (813) 985-5533.

Tampa / Practical Information

Accommodation

Camping: Busch Gardens Travel Park, 146 tent and RV sites, from $18 for five persons, additional person $2, 10001 McKinley Drive, reservations are recommended; Tel: (813) 971-0008.

Tampa East Green Acres Campground, 300 tent and RV sites, $18 to $20 for one and two persons, additional person $2, 12720 US 92 in Plant City/Dover; Tel: (813) 659-0002.

Tampa East Green Acres Travel Park, 264 tent and RV sites, $18 to $22 for four persons, additional person $2, 4630 McIntosh Road in Plant City/Dover, reservations are recommended; Tel: (813) 659-0002.

Tampa East KOA, 170 tent and RV sites, $18 to $20 for two persons, additional person $3, McIntosh Road in Plant City/Dover, reservations are recommended; Tel: (813) 659-2202 and 1-800-872-3562.

Hotels/Motels: Budgetel Inn, Tampa Southeast, 602 South Faulkenburg Road, $45 to $65 for one and two persons, additional person $5; Tel: (813) 684-4007.

Budgetel Inn, 4811 US Highway 301 North, $35 to $55 for one and two persons, additional person $5; Tel: (813) 626-0885.

Days Inn on Rocky Point Island, 7627 Courtney Campbell Causeway, $40 to $65 for one and two persons, additional person $6, free shuttle service to the airport, reservations are recommended; Tel: (813) 884-2000.

Days Inn Bush Gardens North, 701 East Fletcher Avenue, $30 to $50 for one and two persons, additional person $6, reservations are recommended; Tel: (813) 977-1550.

Holiday Inn Downtown Ashley Plaza, 111 West Fortune Street, $80 to $100 for one and two persons, additional person $6 to $8, free shuttle service to the airport, reservations are recommended; Tel: (813) 223-1351.

Economy Inn, 1810 East Busch Boulevard, $35 to $50 for one and two persons, additional person $6; Tel: (813) 933-2665.

Red Roof Inn, 2307 Busch Boulevard, $35 to $50 for one and two persons, additional person $6; Tel: (813) 932-0073.

Red Roof Inn, 5001 North US 301, $35 to $40 for one and two persons, additional person $6; Tel: (813) 623-5245.

Beaches: The Ben T. Davis Municipal Beach is a public and patrolled beach.

Medical Care: For medical assistance and consultation contact Travellers Aid, 205 West Brorein Street; Tel: (813) 253-6064.

Night Life and Entertainment: The entertainment section of the "Tampa Tribune," the largest daily paper in the city or the monthly brochure "See" will offer information on the current entertainment programmes and special events.

Popular bars and clubs are: Confetti, 4811 West Cypress Street (happy hour); Tel: (813) 875-6358. Brothers, Too, Austin Center West, 1408 North Westshore Boulevard; Tel: (813) 879-1926. And finally, Selena's, 1623 Snow Avenue; Tel: (813) 251-2116.

Restaurants: Bern's Steak House, 1208 South Howard Avenue, huge selection of seafood and wines, reservations are recommended; Tel: (813) 251-2421. Crawdaddy's, 2500 Rocky Point Drive, exclusive restaurant with a very nice ambience, reservations are recommended; Tel: (813) 885-7407.

Columbia, 2117 East 7th Avenue, very old restaurant serving Spanish cuisine; Tel: (813) 248-4961.

The Verandah, 5250 West Kennedy Boulevard, exclusive, reservations are recommended; Tel: (813) 876-0168.

Shopping: As previously mentioned under "Sights" (this entry) Ybor Square has numerous shops. In addition, there are a number of shopping centers which are also worth seeing. Among these are: "The Market on Harbour Island," 601 Harbor Island Boulevard; Tel: (813) 223-9898; Franklin Street, between Cass Street and John F. Kennedy Boulevard; and University Square Mall near the University of South Florida.

Sightseeing

Bus Tours: Grey Line; Tel: (813) 273-0845 and (813) 228-9005. One can board the buses at Westshore Mall and Ashley Hotel.

Around the Town Guided Tours, 14009 North Dale Mabry; Tel: (813) 961-4120; Tel: (813) 961-4120.

All Star Tours Corp., 10006 North Dale Mabry, Suite 202, Tampa, Florida 33618; Tel: (813) 968-4274.

American Luxury Motor Coaches, Inc., 1239 East Kennedy Boulevard, Tampa, Florida 33602; Tel: (813) 228-9117.

Five Star Tours, 1211 East Madison Street, Tampa, Florida 33612; Tel: (813) 229-0634.

Boat Tours: Island Adventure Excursion Boat, Ashley Street Dock; Tel: (813) 253-3889.

SeaEscape Cruises, 1-800-432-0900.

Sports and Recreation

Golf: Public golf courses can be found in Rogers Park; Tel: (813) 234-1911; on Rocky Point, 4151 Dana Shores Drive; Tel: (813) 884-5141; and Babe Zaharias, 11412 Forest Hills Drive; Tel: (813) 932-8932.

Dog Races: Tampa Greyhound Track, 8300 Nebraska Avenue; Tel: (813) 932-4313.

Horse Races: Hillsborough Avenue and 12505 Race Track Road; Tel: (813) 855-4401.

Jai-Alai: Tampa Fronton, 5125 South Dale Mabry Highway/Gandy Boulevard; Tel: (813) 831-1411.

Transportation

Trains: Amtrak Station, 601 North Nebraska Avenue; Tel: (813) 229-2473.

Buses: Hart Line is the name of the public bus system. Its network covers the entire city. Information: Tel: (813) 254-4278.

Greyhound Terminal: 610 East Polk Street; Tel: (813) 229-1501.

Continental Trailways Terminal: 501 East Madison; Tel: (813) 229-1831.

Airport: The Tampa International Airport (TPA) is located about 5 miles west of the center of the city; Tel: (813) 276-3400.

Taxi: One or two persons can use a taxi in Tampa for the fare of $1.90 to $2.10 for the first mile and $1 for each additional mile. 25 cents is charged for each additional person.

Important Addresses

Informational materials are available at:

The Greater Tampa Chamber of Commerce, 801 East Kennedy Boulevard; Tel: (813) 228-7777. The office is open from Monday to Friday from 8 am to 5 pm. Other tourist information offices are located at:

715 East Sitka in northern Tampa; 4803 South Himes Avenue in southern Tampa; 3005 West Columbus Drive in western Tampa.

Tampa Convention and Visitors Association, 100 South Ashley Drive, Suite 850, Tampa, Florida 33602; Tel: (813) 223-1111.

Tarpon Springs

Population: 13,000

Around the turn of the century, Greek sponge divers settled in the region around Tarpon Springs, since this area offered excellent conditions for harvesting

---

Walt Disney World is a must for every visitor to Florida — a world of imagination, where everything is possible ▶

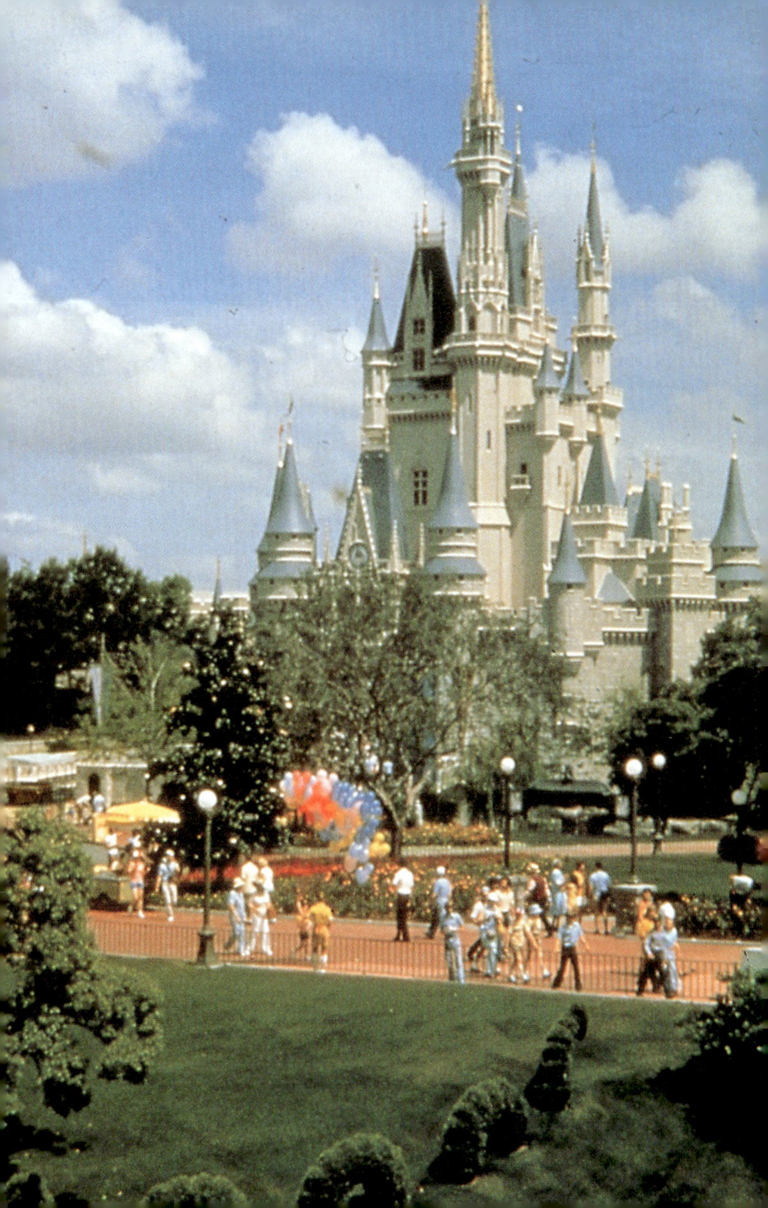

sponges. Although this branch of the economy no longer plays a significant role, the Greek influence on Tarpon Springs has remained, as is also the case with the specific traditions of the sponge divers who once lived in this small harbour town.

Spongeorama Exhibit Center, 510 Dodecanese Boulevard. Here, one will be able to find out everything worth knowing about this formerly prosperous industry; Tel: (813) 937-4111.

St. Nicholas Greek Orthodox Cathedral, 30 North Pinellas Avenue. Not only the building but also the icons, statues and the altar are worth seeing. This is one of the most obvious manifestations of the Greek traditions in this city — especially when cultural festivals take place.

Tarpon Springs / Practical Information
Accommodation
Camping: Caladesi Travel Trailer Park, 86 RV sites, $16 for two persons, additional person $2, 205 Dempsey Road in Palm Harbor, reservations are recommended; Tel: (813) 784-3622.

Palm Harbor Resort, 27 tent and RV sites, from $18, 2119 Alt. 19 North in Palm Harbor, reservations are recommended; Tel: (813) 785-3402.

Bay Aire Travel Trailer Park, 172 tent and RV sites, $18 to $22 for one and two persons, additional person $2, 2242 Alt. 19 in Palm Harbor, reservations are recommended; Tel: (813) 784-4082.

Hotels/Motels: Days Inn, 816 US 19 South, $35 to $50 for one and two persons (depending on the season), additional person $5, reservations are recommended; Tel: (813) 934-0859.

Important Addresses
Informational materials on Tarpon Springs is available from:

Pinellas County Tourist Development Council, Newport Square, 4625 East Bay Drive, Suite 109A, Clearwater, Florida 34624; Tel: (813) 530-6452.

Greater Tarpon Springs Chamber of Commerce, 528 East Tarpon Avenue, Tarpon Springs, Florida 33589; Tel: (813) 937-6100.

Telephones

When placing a long-distance call, one must first dial 1, the area code and the number. If the call is within the same area code, one must dial only the 1 followed by the number. When placing an international call, one must first dial 011 followed by the country code, the city code and the number, leaving off the initial 0 before the city code. Expect to pay around $7 for the first three minutes of an international/overseas call. The first three minutes are charged whether or not they are fully taken advantage of. The country code for the United Kingdom is 44; for Ireland, 353.

Theatre →*Entertainment*

Theft

In general, one will not encounter a high level of theft in Florida, but in large cities and anywhere where it is crowded, one does rim the risk of having one's wallet or bag stolen. There are a number of pick-pockets at the tourist attractions as well.
Preventive Measures:
1. Only carry a small amount of cash or traveller's cheques.
2. It is helpful to have a money pouch or money belt to carry important documents. It is also good to carry money in the front and not the back pocket of trousers.
3. One should write down the numbers of traveller's cheques and credit cards and carry this separately. This will help in expediting the process should something be lost or stolen. In these cases one should contact a bank, savings and loan, or service centres of the credit card companies.
4. One should never leave valuables in the car.
If despite these measures something is stolen, then one should contact the local police.

Time of Day

Florida has two time zones: the largest proportion of the state is on Eastern Time and the northwestern portion of the state including Pensacola and Panama City/Panama City Beach is on Central Time. Eastern time is three hours later than Pacific Time (Los Angeles), two hours later than Mountain Time (Denver), and one hour earlier than Central Time (Chicago and the northwestern portion of Florida). In Florida, it is five hours earlier than in London (Greenwich Time).

Tourist Information

Every city in the United States which profits from tourism has established visitor centers or tourist information offices. These should be the first stop when visiting a city or region because they offer an abundance of information on accommodation, special events and tours. Also available here are city maps, travel route maps and schedules for the public transportation.

Tourist Information

General information on Florida and all of the United States is available free of charge from:

United States Travel and Tourism Administration (USTTA)
14th Street and Constitution Avenue, NW
Washington DC, 20230
Tel: (202) 377-4003.

For information specifically on Florida contact:
Office of Visitor Inquiry
Florida Division of Tourism
126 West Van Buren Street
Tallahassee, Florida 32399-2000
Tel: (904) 487-1462

National Forest Information:
Supervisor's Office
227 North Bronough Street
Suite 4016
Tallahassee, Florida 32301
Tel: (904) 488-6611

Parks and Recreation Information:
Department of Natural Resources
Division of Recreation and Parks
Marjory Stoneman Douglas Building
3900 Commonwealth
Room 613
Tallahassee, Florida 32399
Tel: (904) 488-7326

Information on Hiking:
Florida Trail Association
P.O. Box 13708
Gainesville, Florida 32604
Tel: (904) 378-8823

Additional addresses can be found under individual entries.

Tourist Season

As a general rule, Florida is a travel destination during the entire year, if one has not planned on taking advantage of any given seasonal events. The main tourist season for this state is during the winter months when people flock to Florida to escape this dreary season. Therefore, summer tourists will have the advantage of discounted prices.
→Climate, Clothing

Traditions →History

Traffic Regulations

Detailed information on the specific traffic regulations for the state of Florida can be found in the "Florida Drivers Handbook." This is available from the Department of Highway Safety and Motor Vehicles, Kirkman Building, 2900 Apalachee Parkway, Tallahassee, Florida 32301.
→Automobile Club, Speed Limits, Travel in Florida

Travel Documents

For foreign visitors to the United States from the European Community, a visa is no longer necessary if staying only up to 90 days.

For visits lasting longer, one will need a visa which can be obtained from the US Embassies or General Consulates in one's home country. They will also be able to answer specific questions in regard to other entry requirements in individual cases.

Driving licences from foreign countries are valid in the United States; however, an international driving licence can help in a number of cases like when renting a vehicle or if one should be stopped by the police.
→Travelling in Florida, Insurance

Travel in Florida

By Car or Recreational Vehicle

A trip through Florida by car or camping vehicle offers a high level of independence when compared to travelling by bus, train or airplane. The fact that the infrastructure of Florida is based on the automobile makes a good argument for choosing this form of travel.

Another option which is growing in popularity is to rent a recreational vehicle, which offers a high level of comfort, especially when traversing the extensive regions of Florida.
→Car Rental

By Train
Travelling by train will offer a high level of comfort since the trains are usually equipped with a sleeping car, restaurant car and bar. However, one cannot reach every destination by train although the Amtrak rail network encompasses 25,000 miles of tracks. For a trip in and around Florida, rail travel is less appropriate. Still, the rail routes from New York to Miami and, within Florida, from Tampa to Miami can be recommended.

Amtrak (American Travel on Track) is the National Railway Passenger Corporation. Amtrak offers foreign visitors the US-Railpass valid for 45 days of unlimited travel for $299. In addition, there is also the inexpensive Regional US-Railpass, valid for travel in one of the four zones of the United States: west, central, south and north.

Information is available and reservations can be made by contacting the following number: Tel: 1-800-USA-RAIL.

The following cities are incorporated into the Amtrak rail network:
Jacksonville — Palatka — Deland — Daytona Beach — Sanford — Winter Park — Orlando — Kissimmee — Lakeland — Tampa — Clearwater — St. Petersburg — Waldo — Ocala — Wildwood — Winter Haven — Sebring — Okeechobee — West Palm Beach — Deerfield Beach — Fort Lauderdale — Hollywood — Miami.

Amtrak, 400 North Capital Street, Northwest, Washington, DC 20001; Tel: (202) 383-3000.

By Bus
The time tables for the two large bus lines, Greyhound and Continental Trailways, are so comprehensive in Florida that almost every destination can be reached by bus. Travel passes called the Ameripass or Eaglepass are offered for 7 days ($189), 15 days ($249), and 30 days ($349). The prices for these are substantially less if purchased outside the United States. Information: Tel: 1-800-237-8211.

By Air
Of course, the speediest way to get around is by airplane. However, when travelling over Florida instead of through Florida, one will miss out on seeing

a great deal of the beautiful landscapes of this state. Also, the distances in Florida are not as overwhelming as in other regions of the United States like, for example, the western regions.

Those who decide to use air travel as part of their travel plans should definitely compare prices. Within Florida there is a high level of competition for the most heavily travelled routes, making it possible to find very reasonable airfares. The flight packs offered by a number of airlines are only worth the price if one plans to travel all over the United States. The various packages offered by American Airlines, Delta Airlines, Continental Airlines, Northwest Airlines and US-Air not only vary significantly in price, but also in limitations on travel routes, stop-overs and length of validity. Information on these is available at local travel agencies.

Hitchhiking

Hitchhiking is permitted within Florida, but the opinions regarding this differ greatly. The tendency for hitchhiking is definitely decreasing. Hitchhikers must be prepared for a long wait. The best option is at the truck stops near highways. Here one can ask the truck drivers for a ride. One should, however, not underestimate the dangers associated with hitchhiking, especially when travelling alone.

Travelling to Florida

Direct flights are available from almost every major city in the United States to Miami, Orlando, Ft. Lauderdale and Tampa among other airports. Direct flights arriving from Europe will most likely land in Miami or Orlando.

Prices for flights to Florida vary greatly, making a price comparison not only worth the effort, but almost necessary.

From London, prices vary from season to season, but one can expect to pay around £365 for a return ticket.

For those arriving by car from other states, Interstate 10 makes up the most significant transportation artery from east to west and Interstate 75 from north to south. Interstate 95 is the most important north-south route along the eastern coast of Florida.

Vegetation

Florida has been quite favoured by nature in terms of plant life. In many regions, the lush vegetation is astounding. Plant life alone is a large tourist attraction in Florida. This is not only a result of the diversity of plant life and the vibran-

cy of their colours, but also the seemingly ever present fragrances.
There are a number of botanical gardens all over Florida as well, in which one can see just about every type of tropical plant from all over the globe (→individual entries).
In Everglades National Park, a maze of waterways meanders through the cypress and mangrove swamps through a sea of sawgrass.
The state flower of Florida is, not surprisingly, the orange blossom.

Visas →Travel Documents

Wakulla Springs

Wakulla Springs is a beautiful recreational area south of Tallahassee. Even the drive along the 363 heading south and then on the 267 heading west is a worthwhile experience. The region surrounding the "mysterious spring" — which is what Wakulla means in the Indian's language — is a reflection of the pristine character of Florida's origins. The spring itself is not only teeming but is also the deepest in Florida. Open daily from 8 am until dusk; admission: $2 for drivers and $1 for passengers. A boat tour costs $4 for adults and $2 for children from 6 to 12 years of age. Information and reservations: Wakulla Springs Lodge and Conference Center, 1 Springs Drive, Wakulla Springs, Florida 32305; Tel: (904) 224-5950.

State Parks: Natural Bridge Battlefield, Wakulla Springs Road, Wakulla Springs, Florida 32305; Tel: (904) 925-6216.

Wakulla Springs Edward Ball State Park, Wakulla Springs Road, Wakulla Springs, Florida 32305; Tel: (904) 640-7263.

Accommodation: Wakulla Springs Lodge, 1 Springs Drive, $50 to $80 for one and two persons, additional person $6 to $8, reservations are recommended; Tel: (904) 224-5950.

Walt Disney World Resort

Disney World is situated in Lake Buena Vista, about 20 miles southwest of Orlando near the intersection of Interstate 4 and US 192. Walt Disney created a unique 44 square mile landscape of lagoons which has become the largest tourist attraction in the United States when measured by the number of visitors annually.

The expanses of this theme park also makes it possible to add new attractions. Disney World includes the Magic Kingdom (modelled after Disneyland in California), Epcot Center, the newest attraction the Disney-MGM Studios

Theme Park and of course a number of large hotel complexes, vacation villages and a number of shopping and recreation centers. The ultra-modern monorail connects the two main areas of the Magic Kingdom and Epcot Center, a route covering 13 kilometres.

Magic Kingdom

The world of dreams and illusion in the Magic Kingdom was opened to the public in 1971, making it not only significantly newer than Disneyland in Anaheim/Los Angeles, but laid out much more generously as well. Presently around 50 attractions await visitors. These are subdivided into seven theme "lands." These are: Adventureland, Liberty Square, Frontierland, Main Street USA, Fantasyland, Tomorrowland and Mickey's Birthdayland.

One must allow at least one entire day for a visit to the Magic Kingdom and arrive at the park at 9 am when it opens if at all possible. One should enjoy the most popular attractions first; later there is usually a long wait, which can stifle the "Magic Kingdom experience." The most popular attractions are: the Jungle Cruise, the Haunted Mansion, Big Thunder Mountain Railroad and Space Mountain.

EPCOT Center

EPCOT Center — Experimental Prototype Community of Tomorrow — is a presentation of the world of the future. The planing and construction of EPCOT Center lasted eight years, costing around one billion dollars. It was then opened two miles south of its 11 year old neighbour in the fall of 1982. The entire complex is subdivided into two areas: Future World and the World Showcase.

The trademark of Future World is a 180 foot high aluminium sphere. Around this there is a group of several futuristic buildings in which various topics are presented entertainingly as well as informatively.

The developmental history of communications as well as transportation and a trip into the past are as much a part of the EPCOT experience as are the future forms of civilisation in the oceans and in space. Rounding off this vision of the future is the presentation of food production using high technology. The newest attraction in Future World "The Living Seas" is an artificial ocean containing over 5.5 million gallons of water and home to 6,000 aquatic animals.

In the World Showcase, the second part of EPCOT Center, the countries of Mexico, China, Germany, Italy, Japan, France, Morocco, England, Canada, the US and now also Norway are presented at their cultural and culinary best. Lining the World Showcase Lagoon are miniature cities, which are meant to be representative for the given nation.

The new evening attraction, the "Illumi Nations" show, transforms the countries of the World Showcase into a spectacular rhapsody of laser lights, fountains and fireworks accompanied by classical music.

The EPCOT Center will take at least one entire day to explore as well.

Disney-MGM Studios Theme Park

With this, the newest complex, Disney has brought Hollywood to Florida. The Californian prototype is most obvious by the reproduction of Hollywood Boulevard with its famous Chinese Theater. Other attractions include: the Great Movie Ride (a trip through the world of the film classics) in the above mentioned theater, an elaborate stunt show, the Monster Sound Show, a trip behind the film sets, leading through Catastrophe Canyon — the department for special effects — where filming can be observed live. In addition, visitors are allowed a peek into the animation department and the newest attraction is Star Tours which makes an intergalactic ride to an Ewok Village possible.

Those who need to relax after a visit to these three entertainment giants, need not necessarily leave the Walt Disney World Resort. Within the huge area of the park (Manhattan would fit into this area twice), there are golf courses, tennis courts, swimming pools and lakes for swimming, boating and water skiing. There is also the water adventure areas of River Country and Typhoon Lagoon Theme Park offering opportunity enough for recreation and diversion.

Walt Disney World Resort is open daily. The Magic Kingdom is open from 9 am to 7 pm; EPCOT Center, from 9 am to 8 pm and Disney-MGM Studios, from 9 am to 6 pm. During peak season and weekends, the theme parks remain open until midnight.

Walt Disney World Resort / Practical Information

Accommodation

Camping: Fort Summit Camping Resort, 299 tent and RV sites, from $25 for two persons, heated swimming pool, reservations are recommended, P.O. Box 22182, Lake Buena Vista, from Interstate 4, take exit 23; 1-800-424-4999, within Florida 1-800-424-1880.

Walt Disney's Fort Wilderness Resort and Campground, 1192 tent and RV sites, from $28 for two persons, two heated swimming pools, numerous extras, reservations are recommended, P.O. Box 101000 Lake Buena Vista, Florida 32830-1000, from Interstate 4 via US 192 to the Walt Disney World Resort Entrance; Tel: (407) W-DISNEY.

Walt Disney World East/Kissimmee KOA, 380 tent and RV sites, $18 to $27 for two persons, additional person $4, swimming pool, free transportation to

Walt Disney World, reservations are recommended, P.O. Box 420939, Kissimmee, Florida 32742-0939, from Interstate 4 or US 27 east on the US 192, From the Florida Turnpike, Exit 244; Tel: (407) 396-2400 or1-800-331-1453.

Walt Disney World West KOA, 295 tent and RV sites, $20 to $24 for two persons, additional person $4, heated swimming pool, reservations are recommended, 2727 Frontage Road in Davenport; Tel: (813) 424-1242 or within Florida 1-800-237-7734.

Hotels/Motels: In Walt Disney Village are seven first class hotels: Buena Vista Palace, Grosvenor Resort, The Hilton, Howard Johnson Resort Hotel, Pickett Suite Resort, Hotel Royal Plaza and Travelodge Hotel. Prices for these start around $150.

Less expensive:

Disney's Caribbean Beach Resort, P.O. Box 10,000, Lake Buena Vista, Florida 32830-0100, $65 to $95 for one and two persons; Tel: (407) W-DISNEY.

Those who chose the official Disney World hotels will have the advantage of using transportation free of charge and is given preferred treatment when making reservations in the restaurants and for shows.

Hotel Reservations: Tel: (407) 934-7639.

Admission Prices: The following prices are those which were valid in February of 1990:

1-Day-Ticket for the Magic Kingdom or EPCOT Center or Disney MGM Studios Theme Park:

Adults: $31 + tax = $32.75; children from 3 to 9 years of age: $25 + tax = $24.60.

4-Day-Ticket for all three theme parks:

Adults: $100 + tax = 105.60; children from 3 to 9 years of age: $80 + tax = $84.45.

5-Day-Ticket for all three theme parks:

Adults: $117 + tax = $123.55; children from 3 to 9 years of age: $95 + tax = $100.30.

Included in the prices for the four and five-day tickets is unlimited use of transportation (e.g. the monorail) between the three theme parks. In addition it is not required that these tickets be used consecutive days; these tickets do not lose their validity.

In order to reenter the park on the same day, one must present a valid admission and the hand stamp which one will get upon leaving the park. This rule also applies when visiting other theme parks on the same day.

Admission for the water paradise "Typhoon Lagoon" is $18.55 for adults and $12.19 for children under 10.

Only the four or five-day tickets can be ordered in advance, and take four weeks to process. Address: Walt Disney World Co., Group Sales, P.O. Box 10 0000, Lake Buena Vista, Florida 32830.

Babysitting and Day Care: Qualified personnel will take care of children from 4:30 pm to midnight. For appointments contact:

Disney's Contemporary Resort; Tel: (407) 824-1000 or (407) 824-3038;
Disney's Grand Floridian Beach Resort; Tel: (407) 824-3000 or (407) 824-2985.
Neverland Club in the Polynesian Resort; Tel: (407) 824-2170.

As a rule, children must be between the ages of three and twelve.

Climate: During the summer months, the temperatures can reach up to 98 °F, with a high level of humidity. Rain showers can also be expected. During the winter, temperatures rarely drop under 50 °F and during spring and fall, temperatures range between 70 and 80 °F.

Currency Exchange: The Sun Bank operates three banks within Disney World Resort. These are all open daily from 9 am to 4 pm.

Sun Bank Building in Lake Buena Vista, on Main Street USA, shortly beyond the entrance to the Magic Kingdom, and at the Entrance Plaza to EPCOT Center.

Guest Services: City Hall on Main Street USA, in Spaceship Earth in EPCOT Center and at the Disney-MGM Studios.

Medical Care: In the Magic Kingdom, first aid is available at the Crystal Palace and in EPCOT Center, behind the Odyssey Restaurant. In addition, all of the information centers will be able to assist further.

Night Life: In addition to the numerous night clubs in the Disney World Hotels, Pleasure Island is the main destination for evening entertainment. On this 38 acre island only a foot bridge away from Disney Village Marketplace are the nightclubs "Mannequins Dance Palace," "XZFR Rockin' Rollerdrome," "The Comedy Warehouse," "Neon Armadillo Music Saloon," "Adventurers Club," "Videopolis East" (serving only non-alcoholic beverages) and the "Empress Lilly Riverboat." These are all open from 6 pm to midnight.

Admission to all of the nightclubs: $15.85 for adults and $8.43 for visitors under 18 years of age.

Admission for one nightclub: $6.36.

Post Office: Lake Buena Vista Post Office on State Road 535, near the large intersection.

Restaurants: In addition to the numerous refreshment stands throughout the Walt Disney World Resort, there are also very good to excellent restaurants, some of which are located in the exclusive hotels.

Arthur's, Hotel Plaza Boulevard in Buena Vista Palace, a restaurant for gourmets, ranking among the top ten in Florida, reservations are recommended; Tel: (407) 827-2727 or (407) 827-3333.

The Outback, Hotel Plaza Boulevard in Buena Vista Palace, specialising in steaks and seafood, reservations are recommended; Tel: (407) 827-2727 or (407) 827-3333.

American Vineyards, 1751 Hotel Plaza Boulevard in the Hilton Hotel, very good restaurant, reservations are recommended; Tel: (407) 827-4000.

Benihana Japanese Steakhouse, 1751 Hotel Plaza Boulevard in the Hilton Hotel, excellent Japanese restaurant, reservations are recommended; Tel: (407) 827-4000.

Trader's International Restaurant, Walt Disney World Village in the Travelodge Hotel, good restaurant with a Caribbean atmosphere, reservations are recommended; Tel: (407) 828-2424.

Shopping: In all of the large theme parks, souvenirs in every imaginable form can be purchased. Considered the shopping paradise within the park is the Disney Village Marketplace, located directly on the shores of a lagoon. Over 20 shops have something to offer for every taste.

Swimming: Swimming pools can be found in all of the hotels. But a real adventure awaits visitors at River Country with its water slides, river rapids etc., and at Typhoon Lagoon with the largest inland surfing area in the world.

Transportation

Between the holiday villages and the entertainment complexes, monorails, ferries, boats and shuttle buses take visitors to their destinations.

Important Addresses

Walt Disney World Co., P.O. Box 10040, Lake Buena Vista, Florida 32830-0400; Tel: (407)824-4321.

Travel Industry Relations, The Walt Disney Co., 31-32 Soho Square, London W1V 6AP, England; Tel: 071-734 8111.

Weather →*Climate*

Winter Haven

Population: 21,000

Cypress Gardens in Winter Haven is among the oldest attractions that the state of Florida has to offer. This is not only a fabulous botanical park with cypresses, tropical plants, lakes and caves but also a zoological garden and theme park. Water ski shows, animal shows, comedy acts and much more make a visit to Cypress Gardens a must for those travelling to Florida. One should allow at least six hours for a visit to Cypress Gardens. Open daily from 9 am to 6 pm; longer hours in summer and during weekends. Admission: $18.95 for adults and $12.95 for children from 3 to 9 years of age. Information: Cypress Gardens, P.O. Box 1, Cypress Gardens, Florida 33884; Tel: (813) 324-2111.

Youth Hostels →*Accommodation and individual entries*